Countering the Financing of Terrorism
in the International Community

Ivica Simonovski / Zeynep Ece Ünsal

Countering
the Financing of Terrorism
in the International Community

PETER LANG

Bibliographic Information published by the Deutsche Nationalbibliothek
The Deutsche Nationalbibliothek lists this publication in the Deutsche
Nationalbibliografie; detailed bibliographic data is available online at
http://dnb.d-nb.de.

Library of Congress Cataloging-in-Publication Data
A CIP catalog record for this book has been applied for at the Library of Congress.

Printed by CPI books GmbH, Leck

ISBN 978-3-631-76413-8 (Print)
E-ISBN 978-3-631-76415-2 (E-PDF)
E-ISBN 978-3-631-76416-9 (EPUB)
E-ISBN 978-3-631-76417-6 (MOBI)
DOI 10.3726/b14508

This publication has been peer reviewed.

www.peterlang.com

Table of Contents

Acronyms and Abbreviations

AAOIFI	Accounting and Auditing Organization for Islamic Finance Institutions
AML/CFT	Anti Money Laundering and Counter Financing of Terrorism
APG	Asia/Pacific Group
ARABIC	Islamic, non-royal Ar-Rajhi Banking and Investment Company
ATM	Automated Teller Machine
AQI	Al-Qaida in Iraq
BCCI	Bank of Credit and Commerce International
CDD	Customer Due Diligence
CFSP	Common Foreign and Security Policy
CI-CAD	Inter-American Drug Abuse Control Commission
CTC	Counter Terrorism Committee
CTED	Counter-Terrorism Executive Directorate
DEA	Drug Enforcement Administration
DHKP-C	Revolutionary People's Liberation Party/Front in Turkey
DIB	Dubai Islamic Bank
EAG	Euroasian Group
EC	European Commission
ESAAMLG	Eastern and Southern Africa Anti-Money Laundering Group
ETA	Euskadi Ta Askatasuna
EUROPOL	European Police
EU	European Union
FATF	Financial Action Task Forces
FAI	Unofficial Anarchist Federation
FIU	Financial Intelligence Unit
FTF's	Foreign Terrorist Fighters
FOSF	Friends of Sinn Fein
GAFILAT	Financial Action Task Force of Latin America
GABAC	Task Force on Money Laundering in Central Africa
GIABA	Inter Governmental Action Group against Money Laundering in West Africa

JTJ	Jama'at al-Tawhid wal-Jihad
IBBL	Islamic Bank Bangladesh Limited
IDB	Islamic Development Bank
INTERPOL	International Police
ISIL	Islamic State of Iraq and the Levant, also known as Da'esh or ISIS
IRA	Irish Republican Army
LCB	Lebanese Canadian Bank
MENAFATF	Middle East and North Africa Financial Action Force
MSM	Majlis Shura al-Mujahideen
MONEYVAL	Council of Europe Committee of Experts on the Evaluation of Anti-Money Laundering Measures and the Financing of Terrorism
NCCT	Non-Cooperative Countries and Territories
NSB	Nasser Social Bank
NGO	Non-Governmental Organization
NORAID	the Northern Aid Committee
OAS	Organization of American States
OGBS	Off-Shore Group Banking Supervisory
OIC	Organization of the Islamic Conference
OLAF	European Anti-fraud Office
PEP	Politically Exposed Person
PIRA	Provisional Irish Republican Army
PLS	Profit and Loss Sharing
PKK	Kurdistan Workers Party (Kurdish: Partiya Karkerên Kurdistanê)
RAF	Red Army Faction
STR	Suspicious Transaction Report
SWIFT	Society for Worldwide Interbank Financial Telecommunication
UAE	United Arab Emirates
UN	United Nations
UNSCR	United Nation Security Council Resolution
USA	United States of America
WMD	Weapons of Mass Destruction

10

Introduction

We have to live with the thought that in the next hundred years there will be peace, but also be prepared for war tomorrow. This phrase has a common denominator with terrorism, causing fear, and personal insecurity among citizens, which in fact constitutes its immediate goal.

After the terrorist attacks in the past twenty years, the world cannot live peacefully without worrying about its safety tomorrow. Apart from the other security problems, the world faces the "new normality" embodied in the threat of terrorism and terrorist attack.

Terrorism has evolved in the recent decades and has become an essential threat to international security. Its complexity caused confusion and reflected the disagreement of the experts with regard to its definition. The problem further increases in the situation when the individual, who is regarded as a terrorist by one segment of the society, becomes an idol or a symbol of a freedom fighter in the other segment of society, thus leaving the problem unsolved. But, if we want to tackle this problem, we must accept the anachronistic ways of thinking and paradigms. As mentioned, this problem is complex and requires a multidisciplinary and comprehensive approach.

Terrorism as a form of action takes place in several stages in which a range of activities that require financial means are realized. Here we come to the main motive for writing this book, i.e., to explain the need of terrorist organizations for financial resources as they are the key element and driver for their development and existence. Money is a prerequisite for the realization of all terrorist activities and is often described as an "energy source" or a "bloodstream" of terrorists and terrorist organizations. Funds are needed for the development of organizational infrastructure, recruitment, propaganda, training, planning, and executing of a terrorist attack. This explains the need for long-term and stable sources of funding. Most often, terrorist organizations provide the necessary funds by engaging in legal and illegal activities within their area of operations. Hence, we will classify the sources as legal and illegal. And they can be short-term and long-term. They are accompanied by the international assistance of various individuals (their fans and supporters) and companies, and by countries that sponsor and help terrorist organizations. According to the aforementioned, the sources of funding can be classified in the following way: according to the area, internal and external, and according to the type, legal and illegal. Terrorist organizations do not always need cash. They need weapons, ammunition and technical equipment which cannot be manufactured or purchased in the territory they themselves control. The procurement of such resources requires a complex scheme involving a number of individuals, including members of the terrorist organization, and intermediaries or collaborators who support this process. In this way, they often employ intermediaries (also known as "money mules" in the community of experts) who in the name and on the account of someone else (in favor of the terrorist organization) will procure these necessary resources. The problem is getting more complex when the question arises as to how these resources enter the territory controlled by the terrorist organization. A specific example can be found in the global terrorist organization of the Islamic State of Iraq and the Levant (hereinafter ISIL or Daèsh). This organization declared Caliphate on the part of the territories of Iraq and Syria. Naturally, this territory is rich in oil, so one of the main sources of funding, at the same time stable and long-term, was from the sale of oil. These funds were used to pay the members of the organization, as well as for buying uniforms, weapons, ammunition, and other needs. However, a series of questions arise here that will require in-depth research. How was oil sold? Was it sold in the ISIL-controlled territory or was it exported? Who were the buyers? How was the money transferred? How were the weapons purchased and from who? How were they transported in the ISIL-controlled territory? What are the main routes of these activities? The answer to these questions, complemented by the monitoring of cash flows, will help us in the strategic analysis which should give us a set of measures and actions that need to be taken at national, regional, and global level for successful prevention. Another problem that arises is the monitoring of the money flow. Large amounts of money are needed in order to realize these activities, especially when purchasing weapons. Bearing in mind that the financial system in the area controlled by ISIL was not functional, it is assumed that the financial systems in the neighboring territories and states were used. In this respect, the increased frequency of transactions from/to financial institutions should be subjected to an in-depth analysis by the departments for prevention of money laundering and terrorism financing (hereinafter ML/TF) in financial institutions. Once again, we go back to the need for strategic and tactical analysis that will enable us to implement a set of measures and actions for early identification of suspicious and unusual transactions and activities.

We will not stop here because new actors such as terrorist cells, foreign terrorist fighters, and lone wolves appeared on the scene. Unlike terrorist organizations, the "new" actors have different phenomenology and goal. Hence, the need for financial resources is different. They are decentralized and act independently in all stages, including the financing of their activities. As an illustration, 57% of jihadist cells that have carried out terrorist attacks in Europe in the last 15 years have funded their activities, including the execution of attacks, from legal sources such as salaries, savings, allowed overdrafts, loans, family help, personal funds, and even own businesses. This type of financing does not cause suspicion among the financial and non-financial institutions that have the obligation to undertake measures and actions to prevent terrorism financing and money laundering. These institutions, in accordance with the legal obligations, are obliged to implement the Customer Due Diligence (hereinafter CDD) procedure and identify suspicious or unusual transactions and clients. If they identify such transactions and clients, they are obliged to submit data immediately or as soon as possible on suspicious or unusual transactions to the Financial Intelligence Unit (hereinafter FIU) that is authorized to conduct financial analysis and establish grounds for suspicion of money laundering and terrorism financing. Here, the client identification procedure is of particular importance. It is implemented before a business relationship is established in order to obtain initial information about the client, his financial status, intentions, the geographical region in which he lives, a criminal past, or, in other words, risk categorization is carried out which will help the financial institution when deciding to establish a business relationship with a potential client. Taking into account the aforementioned, the establishment of a system for prevention of ML/TF is crucial in identifying the financial flows leading to terrorism. As already mentioned above, a large percent of the financing of jihadist terrorist cells was through legal sources. Consequently, the question arises as to whether the financial institutions have taken measures and activities to prevent money laundering and terrorism financing, whether they have identified suspicious or unusual transactions, and notified the FIU about this.

One of the key elements in the fight against terrorism is tackling terrorism financing. Identifying and cutting off financial flows will reduce the capacity of terrorist groups for a certain period, limiting their ability to carry out attacks, thereby increasing their operating costs, bringing risk, and uncertainty to their operations. In such circumstances, they will carry out actions exposing their safety shield. Therefore, the fight against terrorism financing should be extensive, including all stakeholders in a society.

The analysis of the financial need and means of financing (source of funding, amount, methods of transferring funds as well as the manner of use) should give an answer whether the measures and actions taken so far in the fight against terrorism and terrorist organizations are applicable and useful in the fight against new actors of terrorism such as lone wolves, foreign terrorist fighters, and terrorist cells.

This book will be divided into three separate chapters. The first chapter is titled *"Know thy terrorist threat"*. One cannot create a successful strategy for combating terrorism financing without knowing the opponent. Oftentimes, the financing of terrorism is identified with the process of money laundering that disguises the sources and origin of funds originating from committing crimes through financial transactions. On the other hand, terrorism financing involves the collection of funds with the intention of using them for committing terrorist activities including terrorist attacks. A common factor is the financial transactions. They should be analyzed in order to determine their origin, movement, and use. Therefore, the legal regulation provides a set of joint measures and actions that are used to prevent money laundering and terrorism financing. However, in order to facilitate this process, it is necessary to know the opponent, i.e., all the actors of terrorism. In order to facilitate the monitoring of financial transactions, as well as to identify suspicious and unusual transactions, this section will explain the need for funding, the financing phases of terrorism (sources of funding, transfer of funds, and use of funds), areas in which terrorist organizations are operating in order to monitor transactions from/to those areas, or around controlled territories (the example with ISIL), and the means of financing (main sources) of terrorist cells, foreign fighters, and lone wolves.

The second chapter of the book titled *"International Response to the Financing of Terrorism"* to explain how the international community reacts the offense of the financing terrorism. As explained in the book, financing terrorism is not a kind of crime that can occur within a single country and that can be solved on its own individual capacity. Terrorist organizations have formed a network all over the world in order to provide the necessary funds for their actions. Crime begins in one country and ends in another, and terrorist organizations are closely monitoring legal differences or legal gaps between states. For this reason, the laws and rules between the states must be realized in harmony and international organizations that are part of many states has a significant role in harmonizing the law between states. This chapter addresses initiatives undertaken within the United Nations (hereinafter UN), the Council of Europe, the European Union (hereinafter EU) and the financial action task force (hereinafter FATF) to combat terrorist financing. What kind of proposals are made by the international institutions and organizations to the states for the prevention of terrorist financing, or the legal gaps identified are examined in this section.

The third chapter of the book titled *"The Role FININT Can Play"* aims to present financial intelligence for the purposes of combating terrorist financing. According to international standards, the FIU is a central body tasked with the gathering, processing, analyzing, and submission of data and information related to the processes of terrorist financing and money laundering. Although in principle these two processes are different, the book will present cases where the money laundering process is used in the process of terrorist financing. As a result, the international community has drawn up many legal documents that bind countries to undertake a set of measures and activities to prevent both processes. Financial and non-financial entities which have an obligation to undertake measures and actions for the prevention of money laundering and terrorist financing have a crucial role in this process, especially in client identification and profiling, and in detecting suspicious and unusual activities that deviate from the client's everyday work.

Chapter I. "Know The Terrorist Threat"

1. Know Your Terrorist Organization

Without having a strategy it is very difficult to defeat our opponent. But, what is the strategy and why is it important in the context of combating terrorism financing? In the scientific and expert field, there are as many definitions of strategy as there are subject determinations of that term. They are dependent upon the objective conditions and the period in which they were created, as well as the subjective views of their authors. In this field, the term strategy can have different meanings: "scientific concept," "doctrine," "war or military discipline," "idea," "roadmap" or "development of a plan." The approach of the strategy as a notion in social phenomena is quite complex and usually depends on both the degree of acquired scientific knowledge and the political interests. From a philosophical point of view, the strategy should include what has happened in the past (as learned lessons), what is today (the current situation), and what is expected in the future (trends). On the basis of these three criteria, the strategy should reflect the overall goals and interests of the state in terms of strengthening national security, as well as supporting international security policy in countering terrorism and it's financing. It should define the threat from which a set of measures and actions for prevention, defense, protection, and processing will be established.

From an etymological point of view, the term *strategy* dates back to the ancient period. The coining of ancient Greek words *"strategos autokrator"* can be loosely translated as *"the skill of the supreme general."* According to the famous Austrian theoretician Erich Eder, there is a linguistic inconsistency regarding the translation. According to him, the complex Greek word "strategos" is translated as *stratus* – "army" and *ago* – "to lead," which as a whole would mean "the art of leading an army" (Eder, 1998). From the perspective of today's threat of terrorism, taking into account the different types of terrorist organizations and the areas in which they operate, the military strategy cannot be fully applicable. Namely, the military component, strategy, and doctrine can be applied depending on the location, positions, and military power of the terrorist organizations. But it must never be applied in urban areas, where the use of military weapons can have major repercussions, material damage, and even human casualties. Here, for example, we can mention the use of military strategy in the fight against the terrorist organizations of Al-Qaeda and the ISIL by the broad American-led [hereinafter United States of America (USA)] coalition against ISIL.[1] In addition to the military goal, the strategy in the fight against ISIL comprises of an additional four measures that should be undertaken by countries:

1. Cutting off the flow of foreign fighters;
2. Stopping the funding;
3. Resolving humanitarian crises in the region; and
4. Dealing with the real situation on the ground.[2]

By identifying the threat of terrorism in all its aspects, the strategy requires a multidisciplinary approach perceiving the problems thoroughly and completely. This requires the involvement of more participants on a national and international level, i.e., by identifying the problem and the level of the threat, we will begin to introduce measures and actions that will precisely determine the role of each participant in order to minimize or completely eliminate them.

James Howcraft, director of the Program on Terrorism and Security Studies at the Marshall European Center for Security Studies, explains the practical approach to terrorist strategy that is focused on ends, ways and means. According to him, the ends are "the goals and tasks of terrorist groups," the ways are "the methods of influence and conviction used by terrorist groups to achieve their objectives," and the means are "the resources and tactics that they should use." (Howcraft, 2016) From this aspect, conversely, we can use the same approach in the preparation of the strategy for combating terrorism financing. Namely, the strategy:

1. Should show us what we want to do;
2. How to do it (measures, actions and coordination); and
3. Which resources are needed to achieve the goal?

For a successful preparation of the strategy for combating terrorism financing, we have to determine and define the level of threat. Since the subject of our analysis is the threat of terrorism, which perpetrators are terrorist organizations, terrorist cells, lone wolves, and foreign terrorist fighters, we must identify our enemy. In the financial sector, there is a procedure for analyzing the client, "CDD Procedure", and in this case we need to determine the type of our enemy, his structure, goal of operation, internal structure, capacity, military, and economic power, area of

---

1   The Global Coalition To Defeat ISIS, Announced of U.S. Department of State for formation of a broad international coalition to defeat ISIS, September 10, 2014, https://www.state.gov/s/seci/.

2   Ibid.

operation, and ways of carrying out attacks and of financing. From the answers to these points, we should identify the weaknesses and vulnerability of the threat in order to set up measures and actions for minimizing or eliminating the threat. These points will be covered in the first chapter in order to obtain data on the threat (in this case, the threat of terrorism), to learn about the needs of terrorist organizations and other involved actors, their goal, internal organization, the areas in which they operate, and the ways of carrying out the attacks. Identifying, tracking, and cutting off the financial flows leading to them will be the ultimate goal of this book.

1.1 Mapping of Terrorist Organization and Ways of Financing Terrorist Organization

In the preparation of the strategy for combating terrorism and its financing, it is particularly important to know the opponents, their positions, and areas of operation. The implemented measures and actions for preventing terrorism financing and money laundering involve analyzing and monitoring suspicious and unusual transactions. From this aspect, the performed transactions or those that should be performed from/to the areas in which the terrorist organizations operate, or the region around them, should be subjected to monitoring and thorough analysis by financial institutions. However, not only transactions but also products that are subject to sale and purchase, and distribution to those regions, should be subjected to analysis. The goal is to determine who will be the end user in both cases. To this end, it is necessary to know the areas in which terrorist organizations operate. Although they differ in their nature and goal, they all need resources to sustain, develop, facilitate, and fund different types of terrorist attacks.

1.1.1 Africa's Active Militant Islamist Groups

The increased number of conflicts and violence caused by the Arab Spring did not leave the area of Central, Eastern, North, and West Africa immune to terrorism. The constant violence in the last decade causes additional concern that terrorism threats could additionally hinder the planned economic development that was very challenging to achieve before that period, thereby contributing to improving political stability by eroding future development. Such a development of events provides fertile ground for the creation of terrorist organizations, which is indicated by the fact that after 2010, and especially after the creation of the terrorist organization ISIL, the number of different terrorist organizations has increased dramatically. (FATF-GIABA-GABAC, 2016)

Tab. 1. List of Major Terrorist Organization in Africa.

Terrorist Organization	Place	Created Before Arab Spring	Created After Arab Spring	Allegiances with	Places of operations
Al-Qaeda in the lands of the Islamic Maghreb (AQIM)	Algeria	1998		-Al-Murabitoun	Algeria, Mali, Mauritania, Morocco, Niger, Tunisia
AL-MOURABITOUN *(Merged by Al-Moulathamoun and MUJAO in 2013)*	Algeria		2013	-Al-Qaeda	Algeria, Mali, Niger, Ivory Coast Burkina Faso South-western Libya
AL-MOUAKAOUNE	West Africa		2012	AQIM and MUJAO	Sahel/Sahara region (Mali)
AL-MOULATHAMOUN	West Africa		2012	-AQIM	Sahel/Sahara region (Mali, Niger and Algeria)
				-MUJAO	
MOUVEMENT POUR L'UNIFICATION ET LE JIHAD EN AFRIQUE DE L'OUSET (MUJAO)	West Africa (Southern Algeria and Northern Mali)		2011	-AQIM	Sahel/Sahara region
ANSAR EDDINE	Mali		2011	-AQIM, -branch Katibat Macina (Mali)	Mali

Terrorist Organization	Place	Created Before Arab Spring	Created After Arab Spring	Allegiances with	Places of operations
ANSARUL MUSLIMINA FI BILADIS SUDAN *Splinted group of Boko Haram*	Nigeria		2012	-AQIM	Nigeria
BOKO HARAM *Splinted in two in 2016*	Nigeria	2002		-AQIM,	North eastern Nigeria, Cameroon, Chad,
				-ISIS	Niger Benin
AL-QAEDA	Afghanistan	1970		Have affiliates and allegiances across the world	All above mentioned
ISLAMIC STATE OF IRAQ AND THE LEVANT (ISIL)	Iraq	1999[a]			North Africa
ANSAR AL-SHARIA BENGHAZI	Libya		2011	-AQIM; -Al-Mourabitoun;	Libya
				-Ansar Al-Sharia (Tunisia), -Ansar al Charia Derna	Tunisia
AL-SHABAAB	Somalia	2006		-AQIM, -Boko Haram, -Hizbul Islam -ISIL	Somalia and Yemen

Source: FATF-GIABA-GABAC (2016)

[a]Its origin dates back to 1999 under the name of 'The Organization of Monotheism and Jihad'. In 2004 it pledged allegiance to Osama Bin Laden changing its

name into AQI. In 2006, after several splits and deaths of leaders of factions it was constituted under a new name: ISI. In 2013, it extended its sphere of activity to Syria under the name of ISIL.

Picture 1. Map of Africa's Active Militant Islamist Groups.

AFRICA'S ACTIVE MILITANT ISLAMIST GROUPS

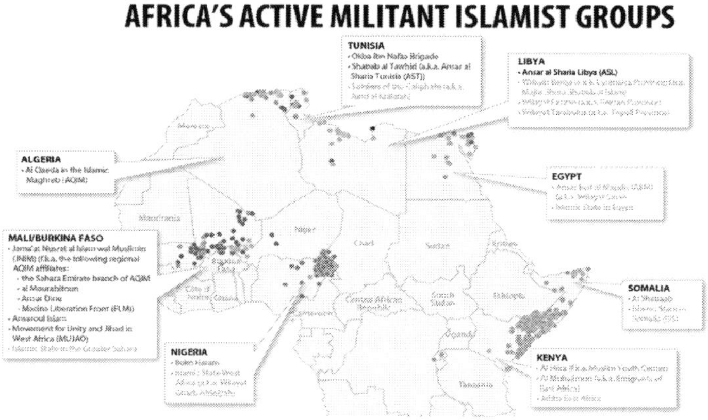

Source: Studies (2017).

As we mentioned above, they are different in nature and have different goals. From the aspect of preventing terrorism financing and undertaking measures and actions, the monitoring of transactions (through a banking system or fast money transfer) from/to these territories is of particular importance, as well as the monitoring of the goods that are transported to these territories. According to the 2016 FATF-GIABA-GABAC report on terrorism financing, the confirmed sources for funding terrorist organizations were the following:

Tab. 2. List of confirmed and suspected and potential sources of funding.

Confirmed	Suspicious and potential
Extortion	Illicit trafficking of drugs, weapons, people, cigarettes, other goods, etc.
Robberies	Smuggling of oil and migrants
Cattle trade	Piracy
Donations	Cybercrime and fraud
Abuse of NGOs	
Local businesses and corporations	
Kidnappings	

Source: FATF-GIABA-GABAC (2016)

The configuration of the African region that is predominantly desert in the central, northern, eastern, and western parts, as well as the porous borders and poor border control, complemented by the still traditional functioning of the cash economy, create favorable conditions for terrorist organizations to raise funds and transfer them anonymously. Under these conditions, cash couriers, or so-called money mules, are often used who have the task of transferring funds to the terrorist organization.

Case Study 1:
Large Amounts of Foreign Currency Physically Transported by a Boko Haram Cash Courier (FATF-GIABA-GABAC, 2016)
At a border crossing, Niger security services apprehended Mr. Z, a national of a West African country, carrying significant amounts of different currencies concealed within goods. Mr. Z was a cash courier, identified by security services as a member of the Boko Haram terrorist group.
The currencies consisted of:

– EUR 568 000 in EUR 500 banknotes (1 136 banknotes)
– USD 460 000 in USD 100 banknotes (4 606 banknotes)
– BHD 135 000 in BHD 20 banknotes (6 750 banknotes).

This equated to over (Communauté Financière Africaine) franc (CFA) 700 million (almost USD 1.2 million) in total. He had travelled several times to Chad as a tourist. Mr. Z was arrested, and the cash seized by authorities.

Due to this situation, the establishment of a system for identifying suspicious transactions related to terrorism financing and for monitoring non-profit organizations and their protection against abuse for the needs of terrorist organizations, such as the creation of an effective cash declaration system, is of particular importance to the countries of this African region. But, nevertheless, this will be futile if there is no trust that should be a stimulator in the exchange of information on a national, regional, and international level.

1.1.2 Middle East's Political/Terrorist or Resistance Movements

Comparing the characteristics of the configuration and the general situation in Africa and the Middle East, there is almost no difference. According to the configuration, the Middle East is mainly characterized by plains and desert lands. The borders between countries are mostly long and are not strictly controlled. In its geostrategic position, the Middle East is a mix of multiethnic structure and is one of the three world regions in which there is constant friction on an ethnic and religious basis, where nationalism and conflicts always lead to massive bloodshed. The other two regions with similar characteristics are the Balkans and the Asian Balkans (Central Asian countries) (Brzezinski, 2006).

Because of these circumstances, in the last thirty years various movements, political parties, and terrorist organizations have been formed, which continue to function, promote their ideology, and carry out terrorist attacks to this day. The world has no consensus about whether these movements and political parties are terrorist organizations or not (HAMAS and HEZBOLLAH being such an example), but they agree and have an identical view when it comes to the terrorist organizations Al-Qaeda and ISIL.

1.1.2.1 Hamas

Political problems between Palestinians and Israel led to the formation in 1987 of the Palestinian Sunni-Islamic political party HAMAS, which in Arabic means "Islamic Resistance Movement." This organization was formed on the principles of Islamic fundamentalism as an offshoot of the militant wing of the Muslim Brotherhood. According to the HAMAS Charter, the goal of this organization is to liberate Palestine from Israeli occupation and to establish an Islamic state in the area that is now Israel, the West Bank and the Gaza Strip. In its structure, HAMAS is comprised of a political and military wing. We already mentioned that the world and the academic community are divided over HAMAS about whether it is a terrorist organization or not. Although it is a complex organization in its structure, the United States (US) (Treasury, 1995), Israel (Mannes, 2003), and Canada (Council, 2014) have designated HAMAS as a terrorist organization, while the EU has designated the HAMAS military wing as a terrorist organization. However, there is one controversial moment here, namely according to the European Court of Justice, the HAMAS military wing has been designated as a terrorist organization based on information obtained from media reports.[3] In addition to these countries, the HAMAS military wing has been designated as a terrorist organization by Egypt, Saudi Arabia, Japan, New

---

3   "EU court keeps Hamas on terrorism list, removes Tamil Tigers." Reuters. 26 July 2017. The lower court had found that the listing was based on media and internet reports rather than decisions by a "competent authority." But the ECJ said such decisions were not required for groups to stay on the list, only for their initial listing, https://www. reuters.com/article/us-eu-palestinians-hamas/eu-court-keeps-hamas-on-terrorism-list-removes-tamil-tigers-idUSKBN1AB0VE, accessed on 05.01.2018.

Zealand, Australia, Jordan, and the United Kingdom (hereinafter UK). While the governments of Iran, Russia, Turkey, China, and Brazil have not designated HAMAS and its military wing as terrorist organizations.

Picture 2. Map of HAMAS Activities.

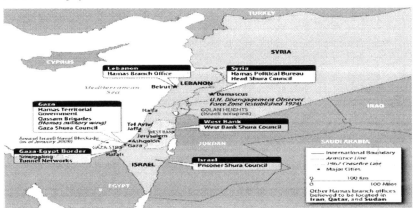

Source: Wikipedia.

1.1.2.2 Hezbollah

The Shi'a Islamist political party Hezbollah, based in Lebanon, divided the world and academic community about whether it is a terrorist organization or not. This organization is comprised of two wings, paramilitary and political. Historically, Hezbollah was founded in order to aggregate a variety of militant Lebanese Shi'a groups under one roof. The project is funded directly by Iran as a resistance to the illegal Israeli invasion of Lebanon and the possibility of its occupation. During the course of its history, Hezbollah was known for its guerrilla warfare, especially until 2000. In recent history, we remember it by the 2012 Burgas bus bombing (Jazeera, 2014).

The status of Hezbollah as a political party, terrorist group, or resistance movement creates confusion in the academic and political public sphere. It is particularly expressed from American or Arab perception. In other words, Hezbollah is a terrorist organization in the eyes of the Western world, and a political movement or resistance movement in the Arab and Muslim world (Shatz, 2004). Russia (Staff, 2015) and China (Nashabe, 2012) have a similar viewpoint. For them, Hezbollah is a political (socio-political) movement, but not a terrorist organization.

Since 2012, Hezbollah has been involved in the Syrian Civil War. Its military forces have made a significant contribution in the war led by Syrian President Bashar Al-Assad against the Syrian opposition (Barnard, 2014). During the conflict, Hezbollah

25

sent several thousand troops to train and assist the government forces in the fight against ISIL (Haidamous, 2015). Of these, about 1,500 lost their lives on the battlefield (BRITEL, 2015). At the same time, Hezbollah was in charge of protecting the Lebanese border, preventing the penetration of militant groups from Syria to Lebanon. According to Hassan Nasrallah's official statement in August 2017 given to local media, "Hezbollah's mission against ISIL is successfully completed, and the Lebanese border is protected from the penetration of militant groups (Sirgany, 2017)."

Picture 3. Map of Hezbollah Forces Against ISIL.

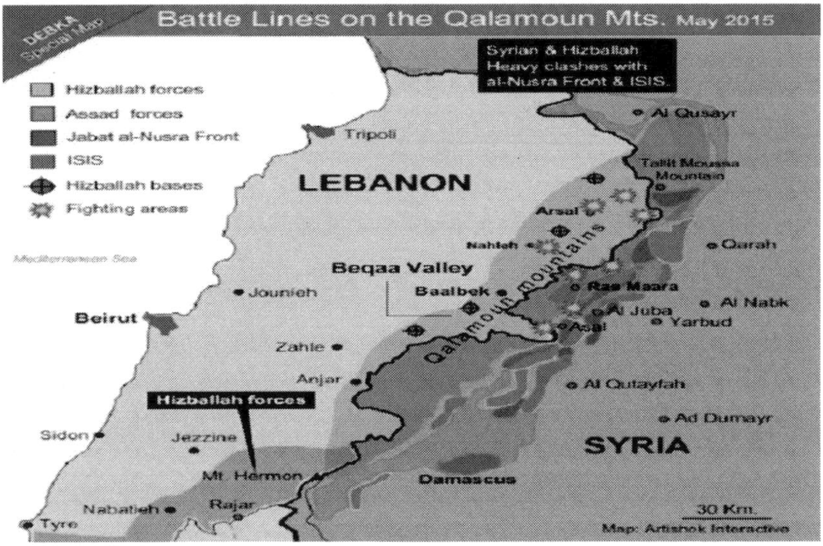

Source: Libnan (2015).

In general, the financing, assistance, and support by Hezbollah are both internal and external. This means that funding does not only involve money, but also arming, training, political, diplomatic, and organizational assistance.

According to Engeland, Hezbollah's main funding comes from Lebanese business communities, private donors, and businessmen who are donating part of their income to this organization (Anissed, 2013). There are also the taxes that are collected from the Lebanese Shia Muslims who live in Lebanon (Matthew, 2015). In addition to this internal funding, assistance, and support, Hezbollah also receives external aid through donations from the diaspora and business investments. In her article, Engeland notes that "Hezbollah receives direct financial aid and support from Iran (Anissed, 2013)."

1.1.2.3 From "Jamaʿat Al-Tawhid Wal-Jihad" to Islamic State of Iraq and the Levant

After the failed military engagement in the Soviet-Afghan War in Afghanistan and after the withdrawal of the Soviet Army, the Jordanian Salafist jihadist Abu Musab Al-Zarqawi returned to Afghanistan, where he established an Islamic militant training camp near the city of Herat. In 1999, he founded the militant jihadist group Jamaʿat al-Tawhid wal-Jihad (hereinafter JTJ), whose followers were trained in the paramilitary training camp near Herat in Afghanistan. During this period, his activities were sponsored by Osama bin Laden (Aaron, 2014). In the period after the US Invasion of Afghanistan, as a response to the September 11, 2001 terrorist attacks Al-Zarqawi left Afghanistan for the Middle East where he had no permanent place of residence. According to the Senate Select Committee on Intelligence on Postwar Findings about Iraq's Weapons of Mass Destruction (hereinafter WMD) programs and links to terrorism, Al-Zarqawi from May to November 2002 was in Baghdad for a medical treatment for the injury he suffered in Afghanistan, and then travelled to Iran and Northeastern Iraq (Intelligence, U. S., 2006). After the invasion of Iraq, Al-Zarqawi and his organization, JTJ, carried out a series of brutal terrorist attacks on Shia religious buildings, civilians, Iraqi state institutions, and forces that attacked Iraq. These events increased his popularity and the interest of foreign fighters to join JTJ in its terrorist activities. Fearing for his popularity in this region, bin Laden in 2004 offered to cooperate with Al-Zarqawi by assimilating JTJ under the name of Tanzim Qaidat al-Jihad fi Bilad al-Rafidayn (commonly known as Al-Qaeda in Iraq (AQI)) (Al-Zarqawi, 2004).

Al-Qaeda leaders urged Al-Zarqawi to stop the brutal violence against the Sunni population, but their attempts were futile. Instead of stopping, he united most of the militant groups under an organization called Majlis Shura al-Mujahideen (hereinafter MSM) headed by AQI. After the death of Al-Zarqawi in the summer of 2006, on October 15, 2006, the Information minister declared the creation of an Islamic State of Iraq (ISI). Abu Omar al-Baghdadi was named as a new emir who announced in April 2013 that he is extending the Islamic State of Iraq to Syria, changing the name of the organization to the Islamic State of Iraq and Al-Sham [commonly known as the ISIL; Islamic State of Iraq and Syria (hereinafter ISIS), and by its Arabic language acronym Daesh]. In 2014, the organization declared a world caliphate and changed its name to Islamic State (IS), headed by a caliph (Lawrence, 2014). As a "Caliphate" it had religious, political, and military authority over all Muslim territories around the world, which was met with harsh reactions and antagonism from Muslim leaders (Mandhai, 2014).

During their rise, many militant groups around the world accepted the Caliphate and joined ISIS, spreading its ideology. The Institute for Economy & Peace in its annual publication "Global Terrorism Index 2015" presents the areas in which ISIS, directly or through federal militant and terrorist groups, realizes the Caliphate (Institute for Economics & Peace, 2015).

Picture 4. ISIS allegiance with militant groups.

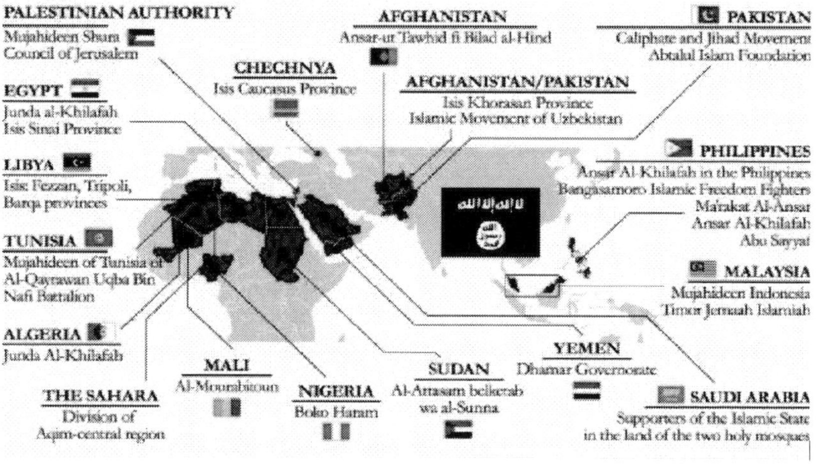

Source: Loulla and Eleftheriou (2015).

1.1.2.3.1 Financing Strategy of ISIL

The financing strategy of ISIL is based on conquest and territorial control over areas rich in natural resources, allowing them financial independence from external sources. The income from the exploitation of natural resources and minerals found in the controlled territory, as well as the systematic extortion of money on various grounds (taxes, fines, etc.) from the population living in that territory provided financial self-sufficiency for ISIL.

In their research, Heisner, Neumann, Holland-McCowan, and Basra note "six different categories of cash inflows into the ISIL account" (Stefan, Peter, John, & Rajan, 2017):

- Taxes and membership fees: These funds are collected from the population living in the controlled territory, as well as from the business community that uses the territory of ISIL for transit of goods, etc. Taxes were also collected from renting out buildings, registering businesses and cars, school taxes, etc (Solomon & Jones, 2015).

- **Exploitation of natural resources:** In order to ensure stable and long-term sources of funding, oil was identified as a key element for ISIL's development. Controlling oil fields in various regions in Syria and Iraq, the annual oil revenue ranged between 0.5 and 1 billion US dollars.
- **Kidnapping for ransom:** Although there are no relevant data on the amount of funds obtained from kidnapping, this type of financing usually does not provide a high income. In 2015, ISIL collected millions of dollars in ransom for a group of around 200 Assyrian Christians it kidnapped in Syria (Hinnant, 2016).
- **Sale of antiquities:** History speaks of many events that occurred in the territory controlled by ISIL. The occupation of many archaeological sites, especially the city of Palmyra, where there are many ancient temples and museums covered with statues, monuments, and other priceless artifacts, was identified as a source of funding (Kareem, 2017). According to Osborn, ISIL had control over 2,500 archaeological sites in Iraq (Osborn, 2015) and 4,500 in Syria (FATF), 2015). There are no precise statistics on inflows after this type of funding.
- **Robberies, confiscations, and fines:** More than $800 million were taken (stolen) from the Central Bank of Iraq and other banks that were located in the controlled territory. Also, with the occupation of territories, ISIL fighters seized and confiscated vehicles, houses, and buildings, as well as luxury goods that were later sold or rented. At the same time, using the strict rules based on the sharia law, ISIL imposed severe punishments for any committed offense (F. Dahmoush al-Mashhour and Syrians for Democracy, 2016).
- **Foreign donations:** According to the UN Report, ISIL "received donations from wealthy businessmen, and religious figures and institutions from the Gulf States (United Nation Security Council, 2016)." There is also the possibility for donations from individuals who provided money through various channels.

1.1.3 Terrorism in Europe

The European continent is one of the few in the world where the threat of terrorism evolves throughout history, especially in the last seventy years. Historically, the threat of terrorism was at the national level within a country. The formation of the nationalist Irish Republican Army (hereinafter IRA) in Ireland, Euskadi Ta Askatasuna (hereinafter ETA) in Spain, the communist Red Brigades in Italy, the far-left Red Army Faction (hereinafter RAF) in Germany, and Kurdistan Workers Party (Kurdish: Partiya Karkerên Kurdistanê) (hereinafter PKK) in

Turkey was generally politically motivated and their activities were related to a specific territory. In the 1970s, terrorists were focused on kidnapping or killing politically exposed persons or businessmen in order to attract attention. One such example is the assassination of the president of the Federal Association of German Industry, Hans Martin Schleyer, by the RAF as a result of their unsuccessful negotiations with the state authorities demanding the release of 11 RAF members from a Stuttgart prison (Wagner, 2017). This example points to two aspects related to terrorism that have changed and are not applied on the European continent today. According the first aspect, the tactics of abducting politically exposed persons and businessmen have been changed by direct attacks on critical infrastructure including civilians as easy targets. The second aspect is the negotiation process. This process almost does not exist in the terrorist activities carried out in the last 15 years. Numerous terrorist attacks were committed on European soil on easy targets where terrorists planted bombs and other improvised explosive devices, used cold or light weapons, or vehicles to drive into a crowd of people killing hundreds of civilians (O"Connor, 2017). These changes came about with the emergence of religiously motivated terrorism and global terrorist groups such as Al-Qaeda and ISIL.

According to the source of motivation, European Police (hereinafter EUROPOL) categorizes terrorist organizations into five groups (EUROPOL, 2016):

- Jihadist terrorism is motivated in whole or in part by a radical interpretation of Islam and the use of violence by its followers and supporters is regarded as a divine duty or sacred deed. In many cases, such organizations have an international character and operate in many countries.
- Ethno-nationalist and separatist terrorist groups and organizations such as the Irish Republican Army (hereinafter IRA), ETA, the PKK and so on, are usually motivated by nationalism, ethnicity, and religion. These organizations usually operate within a particular region in a given country. And their followers are mostly found in the neighboring countries.
- Left-wing terrorist organizations seek to replace the entire political, social, and economic system by introducing a communist or socialist structure and a classless society, and their ideology is often Marxist-Leninist. An example of left-wing terrorist group is the Revolutionary People's Liberation Party/ Front (hereinafter DHKP-C) in Turkey. The agenda of the anarchist organization Unofficial Anarchist Federation (hereinafter FAI) is usually revolutionary, anti-capitalist, and anti-authoritarian.
- Right-wing terrorist organizations and groups are completely different from left-wing terrorist organizations and seek to change the political, social, and

economic system to an extremist right-wing model. The ideological roots of European right-wing terrorist organizations can be a return to National Socialism (Hoffman, 1998).

– Single-issue terrorism is a violence committed in order to change a particular policy or practice within a society. According to the US company for geopolitical analysis, Stratfor, people who carry out independent terrorist attacks are called "grassroots-jihadist," i.e., radicalized people who are not members of a terrorist organization but have been indoctrinated and radicalized through social networks, public media, and literature (Stewart, Setting the Record Straight on Grassroots Jihadism, 2010). These individuals act independently and locally, following the model of leaderless resistance, i.e., they act without a direct command or order from the leadership. According to Scott Stewart, this model of terrorism is not new, and jihadists begin to use it after 2004, following the teachings of the Islamist radical Abu Musab al-Suri (Stewart, 2013). Since 2009, this model has been advocated and applied by Al-Qaeda, which in order to attract new followers and supporters has started its own electronic magazine "Inspire" that in reality is an instruction manual with methods, techniques, and tools for executing terrorist attacks of a smaller scale. According to the magazine "Dabiq" created by the terrorist organization of the Islamic State "ISIL," the instructions for jihadists are to plan and organize the attacks secretly because the less the plan is discussed, the more likely it is that the attack will be realized without any difficulty and problems. Among other things, it is stated that other individuals should not be included in the planning other than those already involved, not to communicate with hesitant individuals, and not to buy complex materials that may indicate doubt. In comparison with terrorist organizations, lone wolves, also called "grassroots-jihadists," themselves plan, prepare, and carry out the attack, which means that the likelihood of identifying these persons is even greater. They themselves observe the target, they procure weapons or make an improvised explosive device, and they carry out the attack.

All types of terrorist organizations, depending on the areas they operate in, are funded by various sources. This work will focus on the still current Provisional Irish Republican Army (hereinafter PIRA) and PKK.

The PIRA used both illegal and legal sources to funds. The PIRA illicit financial sources are coming from fuel smuggling, smuggling of livestock, grain, cattle and pigs, income tax frauds involving the use of false tax exemption certificates, counterfeiting currency, extortion, video and audio piracy, theft of cars, fundraising form the sale of contraband cigarette, rackets, and so on. One of the best known and widely reported illegal sources of funds have come from armed robbery. Additionally, PIRA financing their activity from legal sources which includes funds from salaries and membership fees, collecting by their members and supporters (Oftendal, 2015). Examples for that are support group the Northern Aid Committee (hereinafter NORAID) in US, then support group Friends of Sinn Fein (hereinafter FOSF), voluntary private donations collecting from local pubs and clubs (John & Max, 2007). Also, they created "mini empire" of legitimately – owned businesses. These businesses have included private firms in security sector. Here, the whole operation has become more sophisticated and gentlemanly. Any new company or business to an area controlled by PIRA will be guarded by their security company. These new and legitimate sources of funds have become very popular among the terrorist in North Ireland. In that period, they have had more than sixty security companies (Adams, 1987). Then the "black" taxi cabs (with annual income of about US$ 1 million) hackney cab services, construction firms, a lot of shops, restaurants and pubs in US and Ireland, and courier services and social clubs (Anderson, 1994).

They used multiple methods for moving funds from sources to the final beneficiary and these are usually either through cash couriers, informal transfer system, formal banking, fast money transfer system and high value commodities. The detection of these methods and money flows is extremely difficult. There is a spectrum of methods and flows extending from legitimate sources (e.g., own businesses, salaries, loans, credits, family supports, donations) to illegal activities (drug trafficking, counterfeit goods, financial fraud).

The PKK terrorist organization is a Marxist-Leninist and an ethnic-separatist organization in which Turkey has been fighting for nearly forty years. Even after the under arresting of PKK leader Abdullah Öcalan in 1999, the organization was weakened a little however, today it is continued its attacks actively. A terrorist organization needs serious and long-term financial support to continue its activities for so many years. Because if an organization that has not financial support, it cannot even act its attacks. But also, for the maintenance of the existence of a terrorist organization, they also need other kind of support such as sheltering, logistics, health, and so on. In short, all terrorist organizations need financial resources to be able to continue their existence. PKK, like other terrorist organizations, provides financing from legal and illegal ways.

The PKK's main sources of financing have changed after Öcalan arrested, from state support to other illegal financial sources. Many different studies and have shown that the most important source of income of the PKK is drug trafficking

(Altunok & Denizer, 2009; Ozdemir & Pekgozlu, 2012). Because of Turkey's geographical position which is as a bridge between the "Golden Crescent[4]" and Europe, PKK has used this advantage from the beginning of the organization. According to statistics from the report of the World Report on Narcotics of the United Nations for 2016, Turkey had the second largest heroin seizure in 2014. About synthetic cannabinoids, 5.4 tons of synthetic cannabinoids were seized in 2014 from mainly in Cyprus and Turkey, compared with 1.2 tons in 2013.

Also the same report shows that opiate trafficking on the Balkan route suggests that the majority of the opiates leaving Afghanistan over the period 2009–2012 were smuggled on the Balkan route (through Iran and Turkey via South-Eastern Europe to Western and Central Europe) (UNODC, 2016).

In addition to these data, according Turkey's Interior Minister Süleyman Soylu's speech on 23 January 2017 that one of the most important funding sources of the PKK terrorist organization was drug trafficking and that the PKK earned nearly $1.5 billion annually from drug trafficking (Akgun, 2017). On the other hand, according to a report published by the Police Department in 2013, it was seen that the PKK terrorist organization provided significant funding from drugs and was active at every stage of drug trade. In the same report, it was mentioned that due to its strategic location, Turkey has become a scene of intense drug trafficking between Asia, Europe, Africa, and the Americas. An important part of the drug trafficked in Turkey is used for financing the PKK and other terrorist organizations. In summary, by this report, the PKK

• Received a commission from drug traffickers,
• Control of hemp cultivation in Eastern and South-eastern Anatolia part of Turkey's,
• Coordinating drug trafficking,
• Coordinates drug distribution in Europe, and
• Laundering money that comes from drug trafficking (KOM, 2014).

On the other hand, according to an interview with Osman Öcalan who is the brother of Abdullah Öcalan, the annual income of PKK was $50 million. He said that

"…revenues are coming from aid campaigns in Europe, donations from the people, taxes from companies and businessmen, factories and markets in Syria and Rojava, and customs at the border with Kurdish region," and also stated that PKK did not do any drug trafficking, said, "The Kurds who are drug traffickers in Russia and Armenia are a source of income in their own right. We are getting taxes on the spot……" (Ehmed, 2015).

---

4   Golden Crescent, is the geographical area that made up of Afghanistan, Pakistan, and Iran, where most of the drugs in the global market are produced.

The PKK claims that they did not do drug trafficking however Özkan explains the reasons of this claim by two ways; "first, if the PKK is seen as a drug dealer it may lose its support in Europe and second, if it engages in drug dealing obviously, this may lead its members to use drug, thus degenerating the relations within the organization" (Ozkan, 2016). Nevertheless, it is obvious that the PKK has relation in all levels of narcotics trafficking and it was accepted by the international community including the US government (Ozkan, 2016).

Besides drug trafficking, migrant smuggling and human trafficking, fuel, arms and other smuggling activities can be listed as other financial sources provided by the PKK. Turkey is the transit country for migrating to Europe from the Middle East and Asia due to its geographical position, but the process that started with Afghanistan and Iraq intervention continued with the political instabilities has also increased the mobility of migrants in the region. The PKK utilizes human trafficking to such an extent that it is the PKK's second most profitable illegal activity after drug trafficking. According to one of the big newspaper of Turkey "Sabah", after Syrian civil war, PKK has earned an income between 3 and 6 thousand dollars per person. Considering that approximately 300 thousand people were emigrated to Europe by the help of PKK in 2015, it is seen that how big the income of the PKK has obtained in this way (SABAH, 2015). Since the PKK has already existed on the borders of eastern and south-eastern Anatolia, even if the PKK has not smuggled drugs, weapons or migrants, it has established a taxation system to the region, defined as "custom" and has begun to earn income from this. In other words, the PKK says to illegal organized criminal groups that "you will be taxed if you want to smuggle in my territory" and in this way, the organization get income.

The PKK does not only use this taxation system in smuggling activities. At the same time, PKK collect taxes by forcibly or intentionally from the Kurdish people who live in both Turkey's territory and also live in Europe. In fact, this is not a taxation, this is totally extortion however PKK called is taxation in order to show themselves innocent in the eyes of Kurdish peoples. On the other hand, it is known that the PKK has legal and illegal commercial activities both in Turkey and in Europe. These can be listed as media and publications and commercial and cultural organizations. Money laundering, so-called taxation, and donations are the major extortion mechanisms used by the PKK through the legal identity of these business and cultural organizations in Europe (Ozdemir & Pekgozlu, 2012). For example, according to the estimation of the security units, the terrorist organization derives 65% of its financial resources from its activities in Germany. German internal intelligence organization BfV forecasted the amount of money the PKK collects in Germany in 2015 alone is 13 million euros. It is known that the activities of the PKK in Germany are guided by 4 regional managers responsible for 31 areas determined throughout the country. Also the newspaper Yeni Özgür Politika, known for its proximity to the PKK, continues to broadcast from Neu-Isenburg, near Frankfurt (Perspektif, 2016). The above are just a small sample of the PKK's financial resources. When we consider the activities of the forty-year period, it is possible to find these kinds examples in every source (newspapers, books, and articles). Another factor that needs to be considered here is that the activities of the organization are not limited only to the territory of Turkey. This shows that the PKK is providing external support as well as in every terrorist organization.

It has been known that the PKK terrorist organization had taken continuous and regular support, from other states especially by the neighboring states of Turkey for many years. The fact that Abdullah Ocalan was kidnapped from the city of Damascus in Syria and arrested by Turkish military forces in the embassy of Greece in Kenya had been made clear the support of Greece and Syria. Greece also providing logistical support to the PKK in order to strengthen its position against Turkey in the international arena. "Lavrion Camp," is the first and well-known PKK camp in Greece. The Lavrion camp is the oldest refugee camp in Greece, open for 60 years. The camp, which opened for the refugees who fled the Soviet Union in the Cold War era, became the home of the PKK, who escaped from Turkey's security forces since 1984. When Abdullah Ocalan was arrested, in his questioning process she confessed that the PKK militants had received military training and provided weapons at the Lavrion Camp in Greece (Kemal, 2016; Hurriyet, 2010; Koroglu, 2012; Milliyet, 2013). Syria is leading supporter of PKK by providing shelter for PKK and Abdullah Ocalan till October 16, 1998 either in its capital, Damascus, or in Lebanon's Bekaa valley, then under its physical control. There are several reasons behind Syria's support of the PKK; first the Southeast Anatolia Project of Turkey, which redirected the waters of the Euphrates river second Turkish annexation of Hatay province in 1939 and lastly historical grievances left over from the Ottoman rule (Mannes, 2004).

Beside Greece and Syria, Iranian and Iraq had been direct support to PKK. PKK's main base, which is located on the Qandil Mountains and other main bases of operation and camps in the northern region of Iraq has always been a geographical safe haven for the PKK. Furthermore, Talabani and Barzani groups had given material and weapons support to the PKK. The PKK was supported both during the Iran-Iraq war and first Gulf war because of the fear that Turkey could occupy the Mosul-Kirkuk region. Also, Iran's support of international terrorism is a well-known and proven fact by Western States. There were also several PKK camps in Iran until the end of 1990s however Iran had been never let Turkish armed forces pursue the PKK militants within its borders. The most important reason for Iran to support the PKK is that Turkey is involved in the region as an ally of the US. In addition, the PKK has always carried out its policy in cooperation with Syria and Libya (Ozcan, 1999). It is known beside all these listed neighboring states Russia, the US, and some western European states have supported the PKK to serve their interests of the Middle East in a covert way, but this has not been proved yet (Gunter, 1991).

2. A Need for Financing Terrorist Activities

Knowing the financial needs of modern terrorist groups is the first step in creating a strategy for detecting and preventing the financing of terrorist operations, including the process of executing the final terrorist act. The necessary funds for developing and supporting terrorist operations, as well as for the actual execution of the terrorist attack, are of great importance.

Determining the manner of action of a particular terrorist organization, money is needed to promote the ideology, create terrorist cells in several countries, link them, recruit new members, for training, falsifying documents, living costs (clothing, food, organization of travels, telephones, internet, literature, etc.), financial support to their families, procurement of weapons, as well as the organization of the final attack. Their intention is to keep these activities hidden from the prosecuting authority.

The very nature of financing all operational and associated activities is different depending on the type of terrorist organization. On the one hand, there are terrorist organizations financed by state sponsors of terrorism and, on the other hand, smaller decentralized organizations with independent support that acquire the funding in the area in which they operate by performing activities of legal or illegal nature. In general, the financial needs for maintaining the terrorist organizations, their membership, and activities are quite high. This applies to major terrorist organizations, especially those aimed at controlling and preserving the territories. Therefore, these organizations need stable and long-term sources of funding. Their existence will last as long as they have financial means.

However, the basic feature of modern terrorism is the challenging disclosure and identification of the main sponsors. In practice, the main sponsors are more often different organizations, firms and individuals who acquire financial means in a legal or illegal manner, and much less countries. In addition, terrorist organizations are increasingly developing the self-financing model by providing funding through illegal activities, own businesses or misappropriation of funds from foundations which also serve as a disguise for money laundering. In recent history, an example of abuse of non-profit organizations can be found in France where investigative bodies convicted two persons for raising funds in the amount of 60,000–100,000 EUR through the Pearl of Hope charity. These funds were distributed to terrorists in Syria and Iraq (Bilefsky, 2014).

However, the emergence of new actors of terrorism such as terrorist cells, lone wolves, and foreign terrorist fighters gives a new dimension to the consideration of the financing problem. All of these actors, including terrorist organizations, are different, have different objectives, carry out attacks differently, and thus the manner of financing is different depending on their needs. Therefore, the financing of terrorism must be considered from several aspects. According to the nature of the actors, we will look at terrorism financing from the aspect and point of view of all new actors in the following way:

1. Need for financial resources of a terrorist organization;
2. Need for financial resources of a terrorist cell;
3. Need for financial resources of a lone wolf; and
4. Need for financial resources of a foreign terrorist fighter.

2.1 A Need for Financial Resources of Terrorist Organization

The various actors of terrorism have different needs for realizing their activities. The need for funds of terrorist organizations is different from organization to organization. It depends on their goal, size of the organization (internal structure), and ways of operation. In addition to money needed for funding terrorist activities and providing direct operational support, terrorist organizations need money to finance infrastructure development by promoting ideology as a starting point in the whole process, recruiting new members and training them, and forming a network of terrorist cells in the system. Most often, the recruitment of new members and the spread of ideology are funded through non-governmental organizations (hereinafter NGOs) and media that are owned or under the direct control of terrorist organizations. Today, the internet, social networks, and various blogs for spreading ideology are used more often by posting various videos, guidelines, publications that should contribute to the recruitment of new members. For the realization of these activities, stable and long-term sources of funding are needed.

Comparing the organization's financial needs with those of terrorist cells, or lone wolves, the situation is different. Compared with the sophisticated and complicated terrorist attacks of September 11, 2001, which cost around $500,000 and whose process from planning to execution lasted several years, the process of preparing to execution of attacks by lone wolves or terrorist cells lasts very briefly (several days, weeks, or months). In addition, the funds necessary for the realization of these activities are not significant. Usually they are collected from their own funds obtained in a legal or illegal manner. Most often, these methods are a headache for the investigating authorities' due to the inability to obtain the necessary information about the group, their intent, and the activities they are carrying out. After the loss of their positions, the terrorist organization ISIL publicly called its followers to carry out terrorist attacks in their countries of residence.[5] The ninth edition of their *Rumiyah* magazine provides instructions for ideal weapons and targets for lone wolves (Rumiyah, 2017). Similar instructions were also given by Al-Qaeda published in the 2016 issue of *Inspire* magazine (Inspire Magazine, 2016).

There are many terrorist organizations in the world that differ from each other, starting with the ideology, the way of operating, etc. However, a common thing for all of them is the need for financial resources so that they can achieve their goals. This need for funding is limited to the following:

- **Costs for basic needs and communications**: Recruited persons assigned to carry out a terrorist attack should cover their basic living expenses, both for themselves and for the family or the dependents. Also, conditions should be provided for the person to be able to communicate with the members of his terrorist cell or directly with the terrorist organization.

  The amount of these costs is relatively low but is very important for the realization of the overall process. Since terrorist activities should be carried out skillfully and, above all, unnoticeably, the situation becomes very difficult when operatives do not have a source of funding. This usually applies to operatives that are imported from another country, so the source of their funding is reduced to voluntary donations. In contrast, if the operatives are residents and have a source of funding (salary, savings, credit, etc.), the financing of these activities is done without any major problems.

- **Training, transport and logistics costs**: In order to remain hidden in the home country where the terrorist attack should be carried out, terrorist organizations send their operatives and executioners to train and practice in other countries, usually in those that do not have a legal system or in state sponsors of terrorist organizations.

---

5   EUROPOL made note of this phenomenon in a bulletin: "Lone Actor Attacks – Recent Developments," European Counter Terrorism Centre, EUROPOL, July 20, 2016, for detailed information; s; The FBI has warned of terrorist calls for attacks targeting hospitals, for example. See "Terrorists Call for Attacks on Hospitals, Healthcare Facilities," FIRE LINE: Intelligence for Fire, Rescue and EMS, February 8, 2017, prepared by FBI Directorate of Intelligence, Office of Intelligence and Analysis, for detailed information; https://info.publicintelligence.net/DHS-FBI-NCTC-HospitalAttacks.pdf.

The training of operatives is a very important aspect in the preparatory activities for carrying out the terrorist attack. They need to be carried out by automatism, which means the operative must know exactly what to do in each moment, how to prepare the explosive, how and when to activate it, and all this without psychological fear and panic, in order not to cause attention and to be noticed before the terrorist attack is executed.

The provision of financial resources needed for the training and transport of operatives is most often funded by terrorist organizations that transfer funds through various channels.

- **Costs for maintaining the terrorist network**: We have already mentioned that modern terrorism involves many terrorist organizations led by common ideologies, or organizations that support one another in the realization of all activities. Also, terrorist organizations have their own infrastructure, their own network, which consists of smaller terrorist cells or branches in different regions and states. Maintaining the entire network requires a lot of financial resources. This includes costs of accommodation facilities for terrorist cells, communal expenses for their maintenance, and costs for electronic connection with the other cells and the main organization, etc. From this aspect, these activities can be financed independently from one's own funds or from various funds of the terrorist organization. The goal is to achieve self-funding of these terrorist cells through various sources in order not to be revealed, identified, and linked to the main terrorist organization. As the financial activities of terrorist organizations are monitored by the prosecuting authorities in every state, any direct financial connection with their cells is avoided. Usually they go through intermediaries or alternative transfer methods that will be discussed later.

- **Salaries and allowances**: The funds reserved for salaries and allowances are among the most important expenses of terrorist organizations in order to maintain the spirit, satisfaction and desire of the leadership, and membership and their families. Terrorist organizations are quite attentive to the families of the members of the organization who gave their lives in the service of the organization.

- **Direct costs of terrorist attacks**: The phase of the terrorist attack is carried out after the previous phases are done and all preparatory activities are realized. There is no rulebook for the way and methods of carrying out the terrorist attack. Although we previously mentioned that the two major terrorist organizations Al-Qaeda and ISIL publish special magazines, "Inspire" (Inspire Magazine, 2016) and "Rumiyah," (Rumiyah, 2017) which provide instructions on how to prepare a bomb, an explosive device, and methods and tactics for carrying out attacks and targets of the attack. The main goal of terrorists is to attract public attention through the terrorist attack. The goal of the terrorist organization will be achieved depending on the extent of the effect that the attack will have on the public. For that purpose, the way, place, and time of carrying out the terrorist attack is planned in advance. Most often, terrorist organizations choose objects of a more significant character, or places and areas where there is a large concentration of people. Evidence of this are the latest terrorist attacks on European and American soil where, with the use of vehicles as a primary attack and light and cold weapons, many people were killed and wounded.

Materials and technical means necessary for the execution of the terrorist attack vary depending on the way of execution. For example, it may include vehicles, maps, video and audio equipment, telephones, bombs, explosive materials, weapons, remote controls, etc. If we make an analysis of the costs for carrying out terrorist attacks, we will find that they are very low and insignificant compared to the organization's costs for infrastructure, development, and maintenance.

According to the respected Norwegian Defense Research Establishment, terrorist attacks that have taken place in Europe in the last two decades were estimated to have cost less than 10,000 EUR (Oftendal, 2015).

2.2 The Emergence of New Actors of Terrorism and Their Need for Financial Resources

2.2.1 Financing of Terrorist Cells

If so far terrorist organizations were the main actors, today there are new guys on the theater stage, modern and sophisticated actors who, using all the benefits of globalization and the advanced technique and technology, have become a serious threat to modern societies. Earlier in the text, we saw how terrorist organizations evolve over time under different circumstances. Some of them die out, other dissolve into smaller groups, and some join larger terrorist organizations that share the same or similar ideology. The followers they gain are willing to help them in any way possible. Following their ideology, the supporters are organized into smaller groups forming the so-called "cells" that have a precisely defined and determined task. Some of them continue to convey their ideology, other are in charge of recruiting new followers and members who will join the organization, some are in charge of raising funds, and other for committing terrorist attacks. However, examples throughout history, in particular the attacks carried out by terrorist cells in Europe, show that members of the cells carried out terrorist activities themselves, i.e., they raised funds themselves, educated and trained themselves in the use of firearms, or learned how to make a bomb or improvised explosive device. At the same time, they themselves organized and executed the terrorist attacks.

According to the data, 57% of jihadist terrorist cells in Europe have funded terrorist activities with money from legal sources such as salaries, credits, savings, loans, allowed overdrafts, family help, personal funds, and own businesses (Oftendal, 2015). This type of funding is an advantage for the perpetrators because it is more secure and does not attract attention and suspicion when using the funds. Financial institutions and investigating authorities find it extremely difficult to detect and prevent the self-financing and financing of terrorist activities from legal funds. According to the relevant data available, the individuals who carried out the terrorist attacks had a good reputation among the financial institutions which enabled them easy access to all banking products. On the other hand, the preparation and execution of terrorist attacks in Europe by jihadist terrorist cells did not require large amounts of money. For example, three-quarters of the attacks are estimated to have cost less than 10,000 EUR (Oftendal, 2015).

Fig. 1. Cost of Terrorist Attacks in Europe.

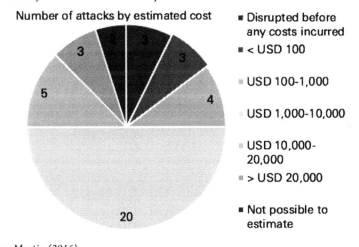

Source: Martin (2016).

The disadvantage of this way of financing is the ample documentation that reveals the person's identity, together with all of his characteristics such as: place of residence, age, criminal background, economic power, physical and psychological features, etc. All these points are subject to analysis by financial institutions, and any unusual or suspicious change or activity will be detected, thereby increasing the risk for the intention of the person to be detected and prevented in time (Biersteke & Eckert, 2008a). But from a terrorist perspective, financing through illegal sources has several advantages, because a large amount of money can be raised in a very short period. Members of terrorist cells are usually opting for minor criminal activities in order not to attract more attention. Usually, they are petty thefts, illegal trade, frauds, etc. These activities allow them to operate outside the jurisdiction of regulators and investigating authorities. But, on the other hand, these illegal activities involve risk and can become more attractive to members of the terrorist cell. Consequently, they may become more interested in making money than fighting for a particular ideology.

Also, for now, no cases have been recorded in which terrorist cells were financed by a state sponsor of terrorism. Such activities are possible to be paid in cash and carried out through intermediaries, with the sole purpose of distancing themselves from the source of funding, in this case, the state.

Terrorist cells are small decentralized units with a membership of 5–10, and a maximum of 15 members, followers or sympathizers of the terrorist organization. Unlike the parent organization, the cells need a lower amount of financial resources needed to carry out the activities, including the terrorist attack. As we previously said, terrorist cells are largely self-financed in order not to cause suspicion among financial institutions and prosecuting authorities. Therefore, they avoid foreign financial aid. Attacks carried out by cells are usually simple and less complex. These attacks involve a small number of people which means a small possibility of error during the attacks, reducing the risk of detection. In contrast, the financing of terrorist cells from foreign and illegal sources involves a large number of people, performing complex schemes and activities that can increase the risk of detection. The "Doctor" cell is a good example showing that self-financing is difficult and sometimes impossible to detect. This cell was composed of three members. All members had university education, good reputation in society, stable economic power and did not have a criminal record. All were doctors in various hospitals in Great Britain (Local, 2012; Taylor, 2008). Their salaries and savings were the main source of funding for the preparatory activities of the attacks. According to the investigation, there is no information on foreign financial aid and international transfers. The chief financier was Bilal Abdulla, one of the members of the cell. Salaries of cell members were transferred to their bank accounts through the formal banking system. The financial reconstruction of the case indicates the difficulty in identifying suspicious transactions, that is to say, the performed transactions did not give any indicator of their plans and ultimate goal (Oftendal, 2015).

Their unusual transactions began 2 to 3 months before the attacks. It was a sufficient time for the bank's anti money laundering and counter terrorism financing (AML/CTF) sector to spot these unusual transactions and monitor their flow in the subsequent period. However, the investigation says no reports of suspicious transactions were submitted by banks to the UK FIU. Their largest expenses were for renting a house that was also a "bomb factory" and buying several vehicles that were used for purchasing the bomb-making materials, for executing the attacks, and for transporting from one location to another. According to the report, the remaining funds were largely withdrawn in cash through an automated teller machine (hereinafter ATM), and the necessary materials were purchased in cash (Oftendal, 2015).

Case "The Doctor Cell"

"On June 29, 2007, two men attempted to detonate two remote controlled car bombs in West London. One of the cars was parked outside a nightclub and the other on a nearby street, possibly in an attempt to target people fleeing from the club. The cars contained homemade bombs made of gas canisters, petrol and nails, which were to be detonated by mobile phones. However, despite repeated attempts by the attackers, the bombs did not explode. The failed attack was soon discovered, and the police began searching for the perpetrators. The two men fled back to Glasgow, Scotland, where they both lived. The following day, June, 30, they drove a car into the terminal building at Glasgow airport in an attempted suicide attack. The car became trapped in the airport terminal doors and again it failed to explode. One of the attackers then sprinkled petrol on the car and himself and ignited it. The car caught fire but did not explode. The two attackers were apprehended, and one of them later died from his injuries.

Members of the Doctor Cell	Costs for:
1. Bilal Abdula	– Gas canisters
– *Iraqi citizen*	– Propane regulator
– *Junior doctor in Scotland hospital*	– Petrol
– *Main source – Salary (1700–2500 GBP)*	– Nails
Savings (5000 GBP)	– Screws
	– Mobile Phones
2. Kafeel Ahmed	– Cars
– *Engineer from India*	– Satellite navigation
– *Return from India two months before attacks*	– Electrical components
– *obtained temporary position at the*	– Electrical items
– *Warrington Hospital in Liverpool*	– Wire rope
	– Tubing
3. Mohammad A.	– Blow lamp
– *Doctor from Jordan*	– Bulbs
– *Senior house officer at University Hospital of*	– Transistors
– *North Staffordshire*	– Walky-talky radios
– *Main source – Salary 4000 GBP*	– House renting
Source: UK	**TOTAL: 16000 GBP**

History tells of another such example similar to the previous one. Namely, in 2000, before the bombing of the Christmas market, during the preparatory activities the members of the Strasbourg cell purchased chemicals for making bombs from more than 50 different pharmacies in Germany (Harris, Burhan, & Connolly, 2002).

Not only in history, but 10 years after the attack in London and Glasgow an Uzbek immigrant in the US carried out a terrorist attack in downtown Manhattan, New York. Namely, 29-year-old Sayfullo Saipov, an employee of the Uber taxi company, who became radicalized in a mosque in Tampa, Florida, following the instructions from the Rumiyah magazine of the terrorist organization ISIL committed an attack with a rented vehicle driving it into a crowd of people (Torsha & Pooja, 2012). Shortly before the attack he rented an apartment in New Jersey, the neighboring city of New York where he was staying and preparing the attack. The attack took place on Halloween just before the New York City Marathon. The purpose of the attack was clear, to cause fear in order to postpone the event. From a financial point of view, the funds for the preparation and execution of the attack were from legal sources (salary – as a driver of Uber taxi). Just before the attack, Sayfullo Saipov moved from Tampa to New Jersey where he rented an apartment and a pickup truck. According to the indicators for detecting suspicious transactions, these payments are not suspicious, but they are unusual. Another problem that may arise in the identification of such transactions is the large number of clients and the number of transactions in the particular bank. From this point of view, the finger cannot be pointed at the bank because there is no obligation to report such unusual transactions to the financial intelligence unit (hereinafter FIU). On the other hand, there is a possibility that the intelligence services made an oversight by not sharing, if they possessed it, or requesting information about the financial expenditures of the natural person (Holly & Dakin, 2017).

2.2.2 The Emergence of Lone Wolves

The so-called Islamic State (territory controlled by the terrorist organization ISIL) often declares itself as the richest terrorist organization in the world (Mc-Cory, 2014). Taking into account its annual budget, we can rightly confirm this fact. The most important sources of revenue are closely related and are located on its territory, thereby making the organization not dependent on foreign aid. Therefore, revenues from donations are insignificant compared to revenues from the controlled territory. But the organization is dependent on resources that are necessary for maintaining control over the whole territory. First of all, it needs a continuous supply of weapons and ammunition to protect its territory. This opens the possibility for cooperation with organized crime groups that will supply the arms. We state this problem several times in this book, how these resources enter the territory despite the military encirclement and the sophisticated technology (satellites, drones) for border surveillance. Although the amounts cannot be precisely determined, according to research data the main sources of income are taxes and fees, oil, looting, fines, sale of antiquities, and kidnapping for ransom. According to the statistics of the International Centre for the Study of Radicalization at the King's College London, the Islamic State's annual budget has been declining year by year (Stefan, Peter, John, & Rajan, 2017).

Tab. 3. Islamic State Income, 2014–2016.

	2014	2015	2016
	(in $m)	(in $m)	(in $m)
Taxes and Fees	300–400	400–800	200–400
Oil	150–450	435–550	200–250
Kidnapping	20–40	Not known	10–30
Antiquities	Not known	Not known	Not known
Foreign Donation	Insignificant	Insignificant	Insignificant
Looting, Confiscation, Fines	500–1,000	200–350	110–190
TOTAL	**970–1,890**	**1,035–1,700**	**520–870**

Source: Stefan, Peter, John, and Rajan (2017)

In parallel with the weakening of economic power, the richest and most notorious terrorist organization began to lose some of the territories it controlled. This is particularly due to the engagement of the broad coalition in the fight against ISIL and the Russian involvement in Syria. In 2017, this terrorist organization lost 70%–80% of the controlled territories under its jurisdiction. This was confirmed by US President Donald Trump who said, "*end of ISIS caliphate is in sight after de facto capital of Raqqa recaptured.*" (Alexandra, 2017)

Following the trend and the risk of total loss, and in order to maintain the strong image it enjoys, ISIL turned to attacks outside its territory by engaging its so-called "lone wolves." Instead of calling their sympathizers, supporters, and members to come to the "Caliphate" in Syria and Iraq, they instructed their followers to stay in their home country and carry out terrorist attacks. The guidelines and instructions for the ways and methods of attack were published in the magazine Rumiyah, especially in the 3rd edition (MEMRI, 2017). These lone wolves are extremely dangerous because they are unpredictable. It's hard to identify them because they do not have foreign help and logistics, helpers, and preparation that could reveal their intentions. It's enough to take a cold weapon in their hands and attack. This method of attack is characteristic of Palestinians who in recent years have attacked Israeli soldiers and immigrants with knives.

Examples of terrorist attacks by lone wolves throughout history: "Alone" wolf Taimour Abdulawahab al-Abdaly died in suicide-bomb in Stockholm on December 2010, after he detonated his explosive devices (Ranstorp, 2011). He used a variety sources to finance his activities before attack. While living in UK, Taimour financed through Centrala studiestodsnamnden (hereinafter CSN) – a Swedish study loan scheme. Through this, he received SEK 745,000 for his studies in UK. After his graduation, Taimour managed to forge university documents pretending to study medical science and enabled him to claim SEK 450,000 fraudulently (Nyheter, 2013). Other source is external sources. Before attack he received bank transfer in amount of 5,000 GBP from Nesserdine Menni from Scotland who was arrested and convicted for financing of terrorist act (sakerhetspolisen, 2014).

The pattern of "alone" wolf Anders Behring Breivik shows different pathways for fundraising and concealment of that funds. In the previous period he established a number of legal persons. He had not been a successful businessman. Some of the businesses were closed, but he never gave up. In 2009 he established company called GEOFARM which was reconstituted as A GEO-FARM. This company was shelter for purchase the materials for preparation explosives. Knowing the fact that he made a bomb which is based on ammonium nitrate, through the company GEOFARM bought fertilizer. According to the characteristics, fertilizer has a large concentration of ammonium nitrate and combined with explosives has devastating effects. Also, he applied to nine different financial institutions for different credit cards totaling NOK 235,000 which he did not used until April 2011. Several months after, several police and military uniforms, badges, weapons, and ammunitions were purchased from different retails in different countries (Norges offentlige utredninger, 2012). These activities were not produced suspicious and Norwegian Police reported that they would not able to detect Braivik following his activities (Norges offentlige utredninger, 2012).

The cited statistics show an increasing trend of the number of terrorist attacks. According to the tactics and way of carrying out the attacks described in the instructions, for the primary attack terrorists use a vehicle that they drive into a

Fig. 2. Lone Actor Attacks and Fatalities 2008-2017.

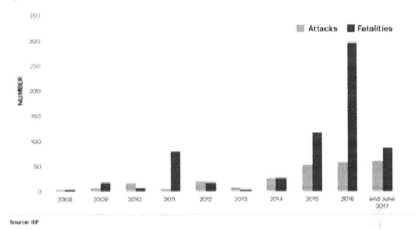

Source: Institute for Economics & Peace (2017)

crowd of people, while for the secondary attack they use light and cold weapons such as pistols, automatic rifles, and knives. This is especially true for the attacks that took place on European and American soil in the period 2015-2017.

In October 2017, Sayfullo Saipov, a native of Uzbekistan, drove a pickup truck into a crowd of pedestrians in Manhattan, New York. In the second attack he used a pistol (Brooke, 2017).

In August of the same year, a vehicle driven by individuals of Moroccan origin rammed into a crowd of people on Barcelona's pedestrian zone, La Rambla, killing at least 13 and injuring more than 80 people (Moore, 2017).

In June of the same year, seven people were killed, and dozens were injured when a vehicle ploughed into pedestrians on the London Bridge. In a secondary attack, terrorists used knives to stab people in Borough Market in London (Harriet, 2017).

A common denominator for all these attacks is that they were committed in the name of ISIL.

2.2.3 The Old-New Phenomenon – Foreign Terrorist Fighters

With the emergence of the terrorist organization of the ISIL on the theater stage, terrorism was enriched by another "old-new phenomenon," the phenomenon of "foreign terrorist fighters" (hereinafter FTF's) "Old" because history speaks of foreign fighters, mercenaries and volunteers, and "new" because the term "FTFs" was first used and defined by the UN Security Council in 2014. This virus has swept the whole world and there is almost no country that is not infected. Embracing the ideology of this terrorist organization, many people joined in its struggle travelling to the battlefields in Syria and Iraq. Some of them financed themselves with their own funds, and others were financed by the organization itself.

Involvement in foreign wars is not a new thing. There are numerous examples in history in which countries have been involved in foreign wars in order to realize and protect their national and strategic interests. The latest example is Russia's involvement in the Syrian Civil War, i.e., in the fight against the terrorist organization ISIS on Syrian territory as a counter- response to the involvement of the US-led coalition. Syria is a part of Russia's strategic interests for access to the Mediterranean Sea. Namely, Russia's only Mediterranean naval base is located in Tartus, Syria. From that aspect we see the justification for Russia's involvement in the Syrian Civil War to protect its strategic interests (Drezner, 2012).

In addition to countries, history also testifies to the participation of mercenaries and volunteers in foreign wars. According to Evan F. Kohlmann, the Afghan-Bosnian network established during the war in Bosnia and Herzegovina and involving already experienced fighters from Afghanistan is especially important (Kohlmann, 2005). Another example of the participation of foreign fighters can be found in the political conflict in Chechnya and Dagestan in the 1990s (Geneva Academy of International Humanitarian Law and Human Rights, 2014).

The term "FTFs" was first mentioned in the UN Security Council Resolution 2178 adopted in 2014. According to this resolution, FTF's are "individuals who travel to a State other than their States of residence or nationality for the purpose of perpetration, planning, or preparation of, or participation in, terrorist acts or the providing or receiving of terrorist training, including in connection with armed conflict."[6]

Various sources speak of the number of FTF's who left to join the Caliphate and fight in Syria on the side of ISIL. Emman El-Badway, Milo Comerford, and Peter Welby argue that "After the terrorist attacks on 11 September 2001, Al-Qaeda numbered about 300 militants, while ISIL by October 2015 numbered about 31,000 fighters on the territory of Iraq and Syria (El-Badawy, Comerford, & Welby, 2015)."

According to a research conducted by two UN Counter Terrorism Center consultants, Professor Hamed el-Said and Mr. Richard Barrett, there is almost no single profile of a FTF (el-Said & Barrett, 2017). As an example we will take the German profile of a FTF's, which does not mean that the same applies to the profile of a foreign fighter in another country on European or global soil.

---

6   Security Council resolution 2178 (2014), preamble para. 9. The term "foreign terrorist fighter" was first mentioned in the Security Council resolution 2170 (2014).

Fig. 3. Profile of German FTF's.

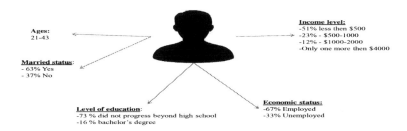

Source: el-Said & Barrett (2017)

As we have said above, there is no single profile of a FTF, but the decision-making process and activities of many FTF's follow one basic plan shown in the table below. From a financial point of view, the FTF needs funding in all the stages he goes through.

Fig. 4. Basic Pattern of Decision Making and Action Phases of FTF's.

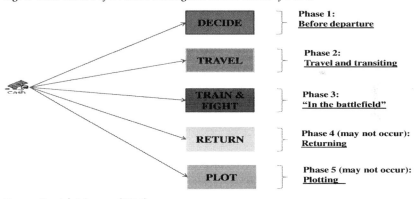

Source: Daniel & Jeremy (2014)

- "Before departure" Phase: The before departure phase is a preparatory phase in which the fighters perform the activities necessary for their departure. It may include shooting training in a shooting club, paintball training, buying camping gear, buying airline tickets for Turkey, renting vehicles for travelling to Turkey, withdrawing cash from ATM's, converting money into US dollars, using "fast transfer" or "Hawala" services to transfer funds to intermediaries in Turkey who need to facilitate their entry in Syria, as well as other necessary activities at this stage. If the abovementioned payments are realized in cash, they cannot be monitored, and the individuals and their intentions cannot be identified and discovered in time. If they are realized through bank cards (debit or credit), they can be monitored by banks and be subject to analysis in order to determine unusual transactions. As we pointed out, this is not about determining suspicious transactions, but unusual transactions that deviate from the everyday financial activities of the persons. According to the source of funding, they can be from legal sources such as salaries, savings, withdrawals of allowed overdrafts from bank cards, and even loans. However, the possibility that the persons can acquire cash through perpetrating minor offenses is not excluded. The first option is safer because the funds come from legitimate sources and do not cause suspicion among the banking sectors that monitor suspicious transactions. While the alternative, the criminal activities, carries the risk that they will be detected and arrested before they realize their intentions.

- "Traveling and Transiting" Phase: According to the location of the country of residence, the FTF can choose different modes of transport to the conflict zone in Iraq and Syria. Due to the speed, the easiest and simplest mode (sometimes the cheapest by using the services of low-cost airlines) is air travel to countries around the conflict zone. According to Fishman, "it is far easier for foreign fighters to enter Syria than it was Iraq (Fishman, 2013)." This is especially true for fighters coming from Europe. They can easily reach Turkey using air, land, or sea travel. Why Turkey? – There are several reasons why Turkey is chosen as a gateway to the Caliphate. First, Turkey does not require visas for European citizens. Second, Turkey is visited by many tourists on a daily basis, and fighters seek alibis and hide themselves as tourists, so it is difficult to identify their intentions. Third, the Turkish-Syrian border is about 900 km long, and it is very difficult to control due to the configuration of the terrain. Hence, the possibility of the presence of facilitators and intermediaries who help the transfer of fighters from Turkish to Syrian territory. From the aspect of identifying unusual transfers, at this stage, the transactions or transfers to persons in Turkey, especially those living in the Turkish-Syrian border region, should be analyzed. The reason is simple – the financial system in the Caliphate is not functional. From that point of view, all transactions to border towns on Turkish territory (Diyarbakir, Adana, Mersin, etc.) should be subject to further analysis and identification of links with ISIL members that support the transit from Turkey to Syria. Also, banks should monitor and analyze payments for the type of transport used by the persons to reach Turkey. Following the payments for renting vehicles, accommodation, fuel, tolls or vignettes, it is possible to determine the main route which persons follow to reach Turkey in order to be transferred to the conflict zone.

- "In the Battlefield" Phase: In the conflict zone, people do not need funding because they receive salary for their membership and activities on behalf of ISIL. If they need additional funds, they can ask members of their families or close friends to send them some. Most often these transactions are intended for intermediaries who cross the Turkish-Syrian border, withdraw the funds, and deliver them to the fighters.
- "Returning" Phase: It cannot be said with certainty that this phase can be realized. Many of the fighters die on the battlefields, while others remain there forever. Many of them may be disillusioned by the situation and desert in order to return to their countries. To that end, they should again go to the neighboring countries where they would organize their return. If they remain without money, they can ask members of their families or close friends to transfer them some. Assuming they are located in the border regions with the conflict zone where the financial system is functional, all transactions to these locations should be subject to deeper analysis and further investigation.
- "Plotting" Phase: Also, this phase may not be realized if the fighter dies, stays there forever, or renounces the ideology of the terrorist organization. If the fighter continues and investigative authorities do not take appropriate measures to prosecute and bring him to justice, he may use legal or illegal sources to finance further activities.

3. Phases of Financing Terrorist Activities

The process of financing terrorist activities takes place in three distinct phases:

Fig. 5. Phases of Financing of Terrorism.

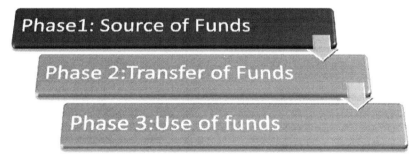

Each phase is carried out through different ways and mechanisms that can be vulnerable to the systems for preventing financing of terrorist activities established by state institutions. We will explain the process of each phase further in the book.

3.1 Sources of Financing

In the previous chapter we pointed out the need of financing in the execution of all phases of terrorism. Generally speaking, the source and way of financing can be legal and illegal. According to the legal source, the financial resources are usually provided through donations from various non-profit organizations, firms, corporations, etc., and also through donations from individuals who share the ideology of the terrorist organization. Donations are the easiest way to provide financial resources in countries where cash flow control is not very rigorous. This includes the phenomenon called "black-washing," according to which funds from legal sources (funds obtained by various projects, welfare payments, and state subsidies) are misused for funding terrorist activities.

Also, using the legal way to obtain money, terrorists often open businesses, hotels, cafes, restaurants, taxi companies, driving schools, etc. These business activities are particularly useful for terrorist organizations because by hiding behind legal activities they provide financial resources for the achievement of their goals. In the event that terrorists cannot provide funds from legal sources, they use alternative ways of securing financial resources mostly through self-financing, criminal activities, state sponsors of terrorism, etc. This is accompanied by the international aid from various individuals (their supporters and followers) and companies to states that sponsor and help terrorist operations. According to the above, the classification of sources of funding can be done in the following way: according to the area, internal and external, and according to the type, legal and illegal.

In the next section, we will specifically explain the legal and illegal sources of securing the financial resources necessary for carrying out all phases of terrorism, but we will also give a brief overview of self-financing as a way of obtaining financial resources.

3.1.1 Illegal Sources of Financing

Following the great pressure of the international community applied through the implementation of mechanisms for preventing and fighting terrorism, the financial support for terrorist organizations received from state sponsors has been completely reduced with the intention of disappearing. From this aspect, the terrorists are forced to find alternative sources for financing their activities in order to achieve their goals. Therefore, terrorists carry out various criminal activities such as arms trafficking, money extortion from hostages, racketeering, drug trafficking, etc., or are connected with organized groups that carry out activities in the area of organized crime and thus provide funding to support terrorist organizations.

The following figure shows the way of securing funds from illegal sources:

Fig. 6.   Illegal Sources of Funds.

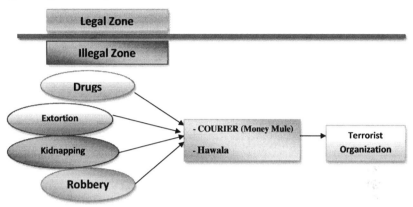

As we can see here, the action takes place in the illegal zone where the bodies for monitoring and supervision of the financial system are not able to take any measures and actions. Terrorists usually choose this way of securing financial resources for the realization of their activities because the money flow cannot be determined by the prosecuting authorities. According to the figure, sources of funding are money from selling drugs, robberies, kidnappings, extortions, etc. The transfer of funds is done through intermediaries who transfer them in cash to the terrorist organization. The method of transferring funds obtained from legal and illegal sources will be discussed in the following chapters.

3.1.1.1 The Connection Between Terrorism and Organized Crime

The international character, considerable mobility, and flexibility in finding new methods of action remain unknown to the prosecuting authorities; hence the difficulty in finding relevant methods for early breaking up of organized crime (Sulejmanov, 2000). Such diversity is increasingly based on symbiosis and unconventional ties between organized crime and terrorist organizations, especially when it comes to providing logistic support to terrorists, i.e., transportation and accommodation. Terrorists and criminals can be bad partners. The determination of the mutual interests of these two groups is one of the most unfortunate consequences of all economic and financial liberalization of the Euro-Atlantic region.

Organized crime knows no bounds. The goal of the criminal organizations is to integrate into the permanent system and the economic institutions, and through various forms of influence to exert pressure on the people from state bodies and institutions who are authorized to give certain permits, lead the economic policy, and decide for larger business deals. They do this by infiltrating their own people in the highest government agencies, by corrupting important officials, etc.

Today, the threat of this extremely dangerous criminality is at a very high level in all spheres of social life, and there is almost no country that is not infected by this type of criminality. By using all means – from those who appear legal to open blackmail, threats, bribery, political, and other ties with particular cruelty, ruthlessness and violence – they commit various crimes that inflict huge damage on particular societies and the international community as a whole.[7]

3.1.1.2 Financing Terrorism Through Money Laundering

The process in which money acquired from criminal activities is placed in the legal and legitimate financial and economic circulation, in the most profitable and proven inflationary manner, is called money "laundering".[8] For this purpose, all financial and commercial opportunities are used for the transfer of this income, its transformation, conversion, or blending with legal transactions (Grurof, 1996). All of this is devised for concealing the true origin, nature, availability, or possession of such income (Rajder, 1995). Money laundering has become a real threat to modern democratic countries, endangering the fundamental values of democracy, human rights, and the rule of law. Using the benefits of globalization and technological innovation, money laundering has expanded its scope of operation. The expansion of criminal activities is directly proportional to the need for protecting economic and financial systems (Taseva, 2003). A worrying fact is the spread of crime beyond national frameworks, giving the

---

7   Underground gangster organizations use all their means – bribery, threat, intimidation, political ties – to achieve their goals and to hinder the functioning of legal mechanisms. They often negotiate and conduct coordinated actions against the forces of organized society. However, organized crime associations often engage in mutual warfare, which usually ends with murder or other crimes. For further information, see: Milutinovic M, Kriminologija, Savremenaadministracija, sestoizdanje-Beograd, Beograd, 1990, str. 237.

8   The etiology of money laundering began sometime in the 1920s when Al Capone's Chicago criminals presented "dirty" money as a daily turnover in newly opened laundromats. In 1945, mobsters Meyer Lansky and Bagsy Siegel used the unlawfully obtained money from prostitution and gambling to buy a hotel in Las Vegas, and since the 1960s money that needs to be "laundered" usually comes from drug trafficking, illegal trade in firearms, works of art, precious metals, human organs, etc. More recently, laundered money originates from tax evasion, fictitious business, etc.

process of money laundering an international character, i.e., it becomes a global problem above all for the financial and economic system of countries.

The problem of financing terrorism through money laundering gained momentum since the September 11 attacks on the World Trade Center in New York, when prosecutors discovered that the financing of the whole process of perpetrating terrorist attacks was done through the banking system, starting from Saudi Arabia, through the Balkans, and to the US. The transition process in countries with a weak legal system enables obtaining criminal incomes through the abuse of payment instruments, insurance frauds, illegal privatizations, use of phantom firms, illicit trade, illegal import and export, credit frauds, etc. In a situation of inefficient financial system, gray market, and unregulated payment system, criminal money crosses the red line that distinguishes the legal from the illegal business, hence this illegal money is invested in illegal businesses or is included in the payment system.

All the variations of money laundering are shown below:

A) <u>Traditional concept</u> – where proceeds derive from a criminal offence (drugs, fraud, forgery, etc.).

Black money — Laundering of criminal proceeds — Laundered money

B) Legally acquired money not filed with the revenue service is black money that will be laundered and become clean again.

Legal money — Legal money before they are laundered — Black money

C) Criminal proceeds are reinvested in new criminal activities.

Black money — Black money

Like all processes, the process of money laundering has several stages:

1. **The first stage (immersion – placement)** begins by moving money into the financial system (bank, savings bank, exchange office, etc.)
2. **The second stage (layering)** involves transferring money through the legal financial system, usually to destinations that are not under the jurisdiction of law enforcement agencies.
3. **The third stage (spin dry) or integration (repatriation)** is a stage in which money is returned to the legal financial system and is mixed with legally acquired assets, is reinvested in new businesses, or some financial crime is committed again.

The overall process of money laundering and the stages it goes through is better explained in the following figure:

Fig. 7. Money Laundering Phases.

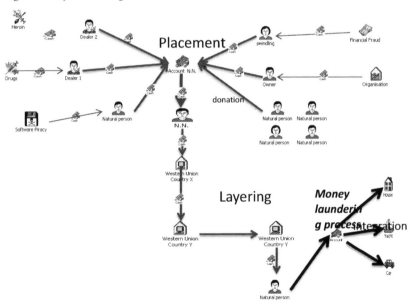

In the following figure we will explain the process of money laundering and terrorism financing. Money obtained from criminal acts (drugs, extortion, kidnapping, and robberies) are placed into the banking system. Here we have the crossing of the red line that we mentioned above. However, when it comes to terrorism financing, we must mention that the funds cross the red line again, but now in the opposite direction from legal to illegal, i.e., a money laundering process is conducted whereby the money obtained from criminal acts, through their placing and withdrawing into/from the banking sector, is used for the ultimate goal of financing a terrorist organization.

Fig. 8. Financing of Terrorist through Money Laundering Process.

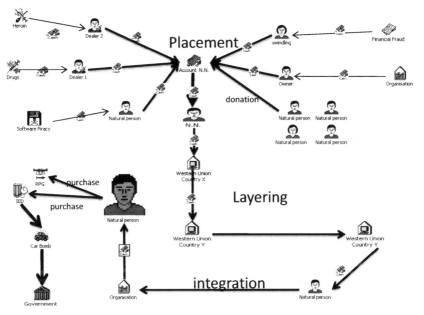

Examples of financing terrorist activities (*according to the Western perception*) through complex money laundering schemes can be found in Hezbollah. In 2011, the US Drug Enforcement Administration (hereinafter DEA) in collaboration with the US Department of Treasury identified money laundering schemes that were realized through the Lebanese Canadian Bank (hereinafter LCB). The funds were used to finance the activities of the Hezbollah organization, which US authorities designated as a terrorist organization. According to the investigation, a criminal group organized the transportation of drugs from South America to Europe and the Middle East through Sahel, West, and Central Africa. Through these activities, the funds were transferred to accounts opened in the LCB through which money was laundered. Some of the funds were laundered through the purchase of used vehicles from Canada and the US and their re-sale (Maltz, 2017).

Picture 5 : Money Laundering Scheme of Hezbollah.

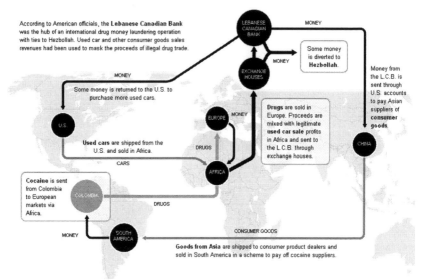

Source: The New York Times (2011).

3.1.2 Legal Sources of Financing

The simplest way to provide money is through self-financing (salaries, savings, loans, etc.), misuse of funds intended for non-profit organizations, donations from companies and individuals, etc.

Fig. 9. New Modus Operandi – Financing of Terrorism through Legal Sources.

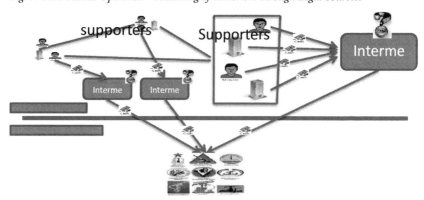

Due to the control of the financial system, and in accordance with international legal instruments for preventing and combating terrorism, terrorists and terrorist organizations cannot open bank accounts. From this aspect, it is very difficult to discover the financial flows that lead to the terrorist organization, for the simple reason that the entire flow of funds goes through intermediaries. And intermediaries are usually non-profit organizations, people, firms, etc.

From the figure we see that there is a legal and illegal zone. In this case, the legal zone is used for collecting money. Money is collected from legal and natural persons who can be cells of the terrorist organization in charge of collecting funds. We also perceive that money is not transferred directly to the terrorist organization, but the money mule[9] account is used as a direct intermediary between donors and terrorist organizations with one goal, not to draw attention and control from the law enforcement.[10] At this stage, the financial flows can be monitored.[11]

Money is withdrawn in cash from the intermediary's account, usually as material costs in order to finance some terrorist activity.

4. Interest-Free (Islamic) Finance Institutions and Banking System

4.1 Historical Roots of Interest-Free (Islamic) Finance Institution and Banking System

The Arabic term "Riba" is a synonym of interest which is used in conventional banking system. Interest-free (Islamic) finance institutions and banking or Participation Banking[12], are those that work in accordance with the interest-free principles in the financial sector and carry out all kinds of financing and banking activities in accordance with these principles. Islam considers money only as a medium of exchange and prohibits charging of any interest. Islamic Banks contribute to the economy of the country using the funds they collect, to the institutions or individuals. Islamic banking refers to a structure that carries out

---

9   A money mule is a person who transfers illegally obtained money between different payment accounts, very often in different countries, on behalf of others.

10 The need to monitor the financial flows and abuse of non-profit organizations for terrorism financing proved to be the weakest point of the anti-terrorism system, contributing to the adoption of the FATF recommendations, an international body whose main goal is developing policies for combating money laundering and terrorism financing.

11 This refers primarily to legal entities (banks, savings banks, exchange offices, real estate agencies, agencies for fast money transfer, etc.) and FIUs.

12 Interest Free Banking, Islamic Banking of Participation Banking are those the same meaning. In this book the term Islamic Banking/Finance will be used.

interest-free banking transactions in the framework of Islamic finance rules. Islamic finance is a system in which all kinds of financial activities and transactions are applied according to in Islamic rules. This understanding of finance has been accepted as an alternative because the "interest" is accepted as "forbidden" according to Islamic religion.

The ideology of today's Islamic finance was born after Second World War, in newly independent India, Muslim intellectuals started to advance an Islamic economics (Polat, 2009). However, the first known successful Islamic Bank was in Kuala Lumpur, the Pilgrims' Administration and Fund (Tabung Hajji) established a few years after Malaysia's independence in 1956. It is an institution that financing finance the hajj[13] and Muslim majority of Malaysian society supported to the idea of the institution also it was supported by the government at that time. TH operates as an alternative financial institution providing halal investment opportunities to Malaysian Muslim depositors. On the other hand, in Egypt in 1963, Ahmed an-Najjar founded Mit Ghamr Saving Bank, a bank based on the German savings bank model. Ahmed an-Najjar was a German-trained Egyptian banker and impressed German savings bank model when he was done his Ph.D. in Germany The Bank did not reference to Islam, it earned profits through direct partnerships with industry and other profit-sharing enterprises, and never paying interest (Terrell, 2007). However, in 1967 Mit Ghamr Saving Bank was closed due to the political reason. In 1971 Nasser Social Bank (hereinafter NSB) was established by government instead of the Mit Ghamr Saving Bank in Egypt because An-Najjar's bank had been popular among the poorer elements of Egyptian society. On the other hand, foreign ministers of Islamic countries gathered in Jeddah in 1970; invited all Islamic countries to promote and strengthen economic business unity within the framework of Islamic principles. This development also effected the Egypt government to establish NSB. In 1974 with the support of the Saudi-backed Organization of the Islamic Conference (OIC) commissioned suggested to establish Islamic Development Bank (IDB) and it was founded in Jeddah. The IDB was considered to be the first international Islamic bank that was established, albeit in part, by members of the OIC. (Polat, 2009; Alharbi, 2015).

The Dubai Islamic Bank (DIB), considered to be the first modern, private Islamic bank, was established as a joint stock company in 1975 by a successful local entrepreneur with ties to the ruling family of Dubai. During the next 10 years, Islamic banking spread throughout the Middle East and Kuwait Finance

---

13 Hajj means visiting Mecca for special dates for muslim population.

House (1977), Faisal Islamic Bank of Egypt (1977), Islamic Bank of Sudan (1977), Jordan Islamic Bank of Finance and Investment (1978), Bahrain Islamic Bank (1978), and International Islamic Bank for Investment and Development in Egypt (1980) was established. After his bank's closure, an-Najjar travelled to Sudan, Germany, Saudi Arabia, the United Arab Emirates (hereinafter UAE), and Malaysia promoting Islamic banking, and in the 1980s most of the Muslim countries like Iran, Sudan, and Pakistan restructured of the financial system according to Islamic principles. Another important development in the 1980s is the establishment of two private groups of companies; Dar al-maal al-Islam in 1981 and Al-Baraka group in 1982. The Dar al-Maal al-Islami (House of Islamic Funds), or DMI, was the center of Prince Muhammad empire, and he established the international network known as the Faisal Group, comprising all or part of the Jordan Islamic Bank, the Faisal Islamic Bank of Sudan, and Faisal Finance House in Turkey. Today the group comprises of three main business sectors: Islamic banking, Islamic investment, and Islamic insurance. Al-Baraka Investment and Development Company was established by Saleh Kamel in 1982. The company opened its first branches in Saudi Arabia but quickly extended its interests to other Arab and Islamic markets. By 1984, Albaraka had opened a bank in Sudan, and by the end of the 1980s Albaraka banks had been established in Algeria, Jordan, Lebanon, Bahrain, Egypt, Malaysia, South Africa, London, and, in 1991, in Pakistan. These banks, while owned by Dallah Albaraka Group, which is one of the leading, privately held conglomerates in Saudi Arabia. Dallah Albaraka groups its operations into three primary categories: Finance, Business, and Media (Alharbi, 2015; Terrell, 2007).

Although these banks, which are summarized above, made financial transactions according to Islamic rules or Sharia, there is no explicit reference to Islam in the names or charters of the institutions. For example, in NSB, the government supported such Islamic principles as interest-free financing and zakat (alms-giving), charging the bank with accepting voluntary zakat and distributing it according to sharia but there was no an Islamic reference in the bank's name and charter. On the other hand, the situation is also similar in Saudi Arabia, if a bank was accepted as "Islamic", it would be de facto recognition that all other banks in Saudi Arabia are "un-Islamic". Although officially all banks are classified as Islamic, non-royal Ar-Rajhi Banking and Investment Company (ARABIC), authorized in 1985 to conduct interest-free banking, is forbidden to use the word Islamic in its name. Today in Islamic banking system every bank has Shari'a Boards who manage and audit the compatibility of the both the bank administration and its transactions to Islamic rules. However, both the DIB and

IDB had been established without Shari'a boards – at the time there was not a manual or clear understanding of how a Shari'a-compliant large-scale bank should operate. The activities of both banks were all Shari'a-compliant, but only in 1999 did the DIB establish its own Shari'a council, and the IDB waited until 2003 (Terrell, 2007). As a result of these rapid developments in that period, in many countries, the understanding of interest-free system has accepted itself. Along with these developments, "According to a survey conducted by the Islamic Banking Association in 2000, Islamic banks operate in 550 institutions around the world. These countries include countries such as America, England, and Switzerland" (Karapınar, 2003).

4.2 Tools of Interest-Free (Islamic) Finance Institution and Banking System

The main principle of Islamic Banking is being interest free. In Islamic Banking, though Riba is prohibited but equity-based returns on investment are accepted. This means that, Islamic Banking uses the profit and loss sharing (hereinafter PLS) system whereby the bank and the borrower make an agreement on how to divide the share of profits or burden of losses for a financed enterprise. Most of the Islamic banks follow the accounting standards prescribed by Accounting and Auditing Organization for Islamic Finance Institutions[14] (hereinafter AAOIFI).

Two main rule of this principle are:

• When the banks perform collecting of funds, they accept the funds based on PLS and not being in the commitment of the customer to fixed income,
• Banks do not give the loan in cash, instead they buy the goods that the customer needs from the seller, to sell the goods to the customer as futures, or to establish partnership with the business owner on a project basis.

Participation banks undertake to manage the money that they collect like a merchant, and to share profits to be obtained as a result of the business with its shareholders.

---

14 AAOIFI, established in 1991 and based in Bahrain, is the leading international not-for-profit organization primarily responsible for development and issuance of standards for the global Islamic finance industry. For a detailed information visit http://aaoifi. com/?lang=en.

Fig. 10. Prohibition in Islamic Financial System.

Fig. 11. Difference Between Conventional Banking and Islamic Banking Systems.

Conventional Banking System

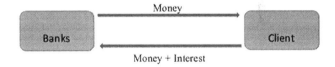

Islamic Banking System

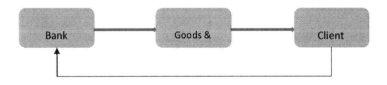

Fig. 12. Main Islamic Finance Tools.

Musharakah (Sharing):
It is PLS arrangement or a participatory mode in Islamic Banking. It is a partnership or a joint enterprise in which profit or loss of a joint venture is shared by the partners in pre-determined proportions. All partners are entitled to engage in management of the enterprise unless there is an alternate agreement among all the partners. Cash or commodities may be contributed as share capital in a musharakah contract. Profits are shared by the parties based on a pre-agreed ratio while losses are shared based on the equity participation by the parties as Islam says one cannot lose what he did not contribute. Management of the venture can be either by all or by one partner. A partner may leave a musharakah merely by giving written notice to the other partners. Although this can be used to completely dissolve the musharakah this need not be the case if the other partners wish to continue the enterprise. If there is a dispute as to the value of the departing partner's shares, he may compel the other partners to liquidate and distribute all assets.

Fig. 13. *Musharakah System.*

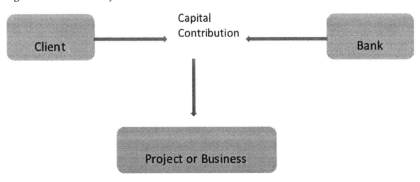

Mudarabah (Special Profit Sharing):

It is a contractual partnership for profit/loss sharing in which one partner serves as the investor (known as rabb-ul-maal) and only provides the capital and the other partner is the entrepreneur (known as mudarib) and provides the management and labor. The profits will shared on pre-agreed ratio but unlike a musharakah, the investor is excluded from management, the sole responsibility of the entrepreneur. Although the ratio of profit sharing is established in the contract, unlike a musharakah, the investor suffers any and all losses. The logic behind this difference is that should the enterprise fail the entrepreneur's labor will have been fruitless and constitutes his share of loss.

Fig. 14. *Mudarabah System.*

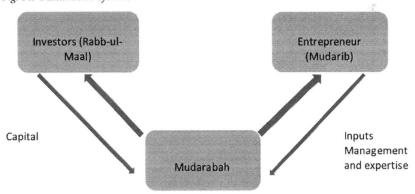

Murabaha (Cost-Plus Financing):

Murabaha, the most widely used of all the Shari'a-compliant financial instruments in Islamic banking is a term of Islamic fiqh[15]. It is a contract of sale between the Islamic banks and the clients. Under this contract, the banks buy an asset on behalf of the client and then sell it to them for a price plus an agreed profit for the banks. It is also known as mark-up or cost-plus pricing. Repayment by the client is made in the form of installments. Murabaha is most commonly financial operation used by the Islamic banks with which they earn their profits and are able to prohibit payments of interest according to Islamic Law. In its original Islamic connotation, murabaha was simply a sale, its distinguishing feature being the disclosure of the cost and profit to the buyer. Additionally, payment may be deferred, the seller can assess penalties for late payment (but they must be donated to charities), and a promissory note or bill of exchange signed by the buyer can only be sold at its face value. Because Murabaha is the most widely used of financial transaction, it has some important rules like subject of sale must be existing at the time of sale and it must be in the ownership of the seller at the time of sale. The sale must be instant and absolute. So, a sale attributed to a future date or a sale contingent on a future event is void. One of the important rules is also the subject of sale should not be a thing which is not used except for haram (forbidden) purposes, like pork, wine, etc.

Fig. 15. Murabah System.

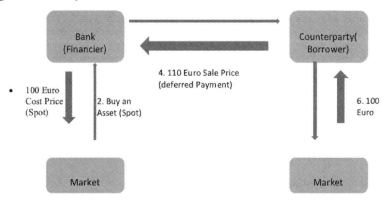

---

15 Fqih means in English "true understanding". But in Islamic terms, Fqih is making rulings and judgments from evidence found in the Shariah, that is, the Quran and Sunnah, and from consensus of Islamic scholars. Fqih is used to create laws for matters not specifically addressed by the Shariah. Shariah cannot be changed. But Fqih can change based on new information. Shariah is broad and general. Fqih focuses on narrow and specific issues.

Takaful (Insurance):
Conventional insurance is also forbidden in Islam, because of the excessive risk and uncertainty involved in most insurance instruments. *Takaful* is an alternative form of insurance that is commonly referred to as Islamic Insurance. Takaful is based on the principle of cooperation and separation between operations of shareholders and the funds. In other words, it takes a large group of people and pools them together to create group insurance. Therefore, the ownership of takaful fund and operations are passed to the policyholders. The policyholders are joint investors with the takaful operator who acts as a manager for policyholders. The idea is that individual insurance is based on the uncertain, but with many people certain statistical outcomes are almost guaranteed. This removes uncertainty from the equation and is a way to effectively manage and mitigate risk. All policyholders agree to guarantee each other and contribute to a pool of funds (takaful fund) instead of paying premiums. Any claims made would be met out of the fund and surpluses will be distributed among policyholders. Takaful operator would be paid a fee only for managing the fund and covering the costs.

Fig. 16. Takaful System.

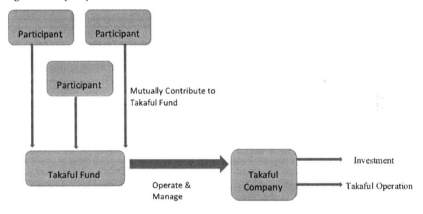

Ijarah (Leasing):
Ijarah is another term of Islamic fqih that means "to give something on rent," that means it is a lease agreement between the Islamic bank and its client. The Ijarah contract is essentially of the same design as an installment leasing agreement. The bank would buy an asset as per the client and allow the client to use the asset for a specified lease period and a lease fee. However, the asset remains in the bank's name and the profit margin is disclosed in advance. Leasing under

Ijarah is similar to conventional leasing whereby the lessee pays rent to the lessor for the usufruct of an inconsumable asset. The asset may be sold in a secondary market, but with it goes the rights and responsibility of ownership of the asset. Rights to the rent alone cannot be sold. Finally, and most importantly, the object being leased must be owned by the lessor.

Fig. 17. Ijarah System.

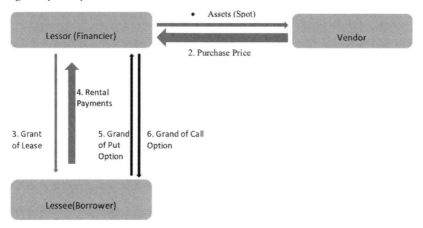

Qard Hasan (Benevolent Loan):
An interest-free loan given for either welfare purposes or for fulfilling short-term funding requirements. Islamic banks lend loans based on goodwill. In other words, it is a virtuous loan that is interest-free and extended on goodwill basis, mainly for welfare purposes. The loan is payable on demand and repayment is obligatory. The borrower is required to pay only the amount that has borrowed. But if a debtor is in difficulty, the lender/creditor is expected to extend time or even to voluntarily waive repayment of the whole or a part of the loan amount. Islam allows loan as a form of social service among the rich to help the poor and those who needs financial assistance. Qard Hasan system offers an interest-free loan given for either welfare purposes or for fulfilling short-term funding requirements. Qard Hasan may be viewed as something between giving charity or gift and giving a loan (qard). Also, a debtor may voluntarily choose to pay an extra amount to the lender/creditor over the principal amount borrowed (without promising it) as a token of appreciation but this is totally depending on will of debtor. In some cases, debtors could make a donation to a charity with this extra amount of money.

Sukuk (Islamic Bonds Issue):
Sukukis an asset-backed bond or an Islamic equivalent bond. It is one of the most common Islamic financial instruments. A sukuk allows asset monetization or securitization and the investor of sukuk shall get a share of an asset along with the cash flows and the risk, and companies form a special purpose vehicle under which it sells its assets. Sukuk holders become shareholders. As interest-bearing bond structure is not permissible, the investor shall get a proportionate ownership in tangible asset of the project. According to the AAOIFI (AAOIFI, 2017) Sharia Standard 17; there is 14 different types of sukuk. Some of these are Sukuk Ijarah, Sukuk Musharakah, or Sukuk Mudarabah.

Fig. 18. Sukuk System.

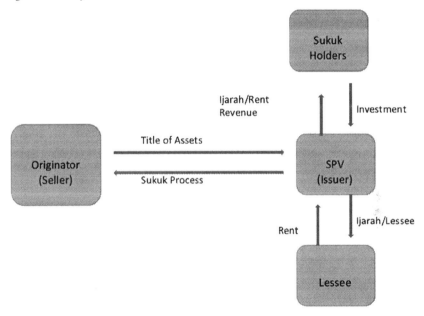

Wadiah (Saving Account):
Wadiah is a contract between the owner of goods and trustee of the goods. This contract protects the goods from being stolen and ensure the safety of goods. Mostly the goods in here are money. It is the acceptance of the sum of money for safekeeping which will be repaid. Bank is the keeper and trustee of funds and liable for safekeeping of funds and returning them to the demand of the customer. In other words,

customers may withdraw their money at any time. Banks at its discretion could reward the customers (hibah) as an appreciation for keeping the funds with the banks.

Salam (Payment for Future Delivery):
Salam is a forward financing transaction, where the bank pays in advance for buying specified assets, which the seller will supply on a pre-agreed date. Salam is one of the two exceptions to the rules regarding the existence and possession of a commodity prior to entering a contract to sell it. In a salam transaction, a buyer pays an increased price at spot in return for specific goods to be delivered at a future date. It is similar to a forward sale contract of the conventional banking system in which the payment is made in advance and the goods are delivered at a specified date in the future. However, the issue in exchange for the advance payment of the price should not in itself be money. According to the general principle of the Shariah that does not permit the sale of a commodity which is not in the possession of the seller, but the Prophet Muhammad permitted this kind of sale after he prohibited riba so that especially farmers – this mode of financing is often used in the agricultural sector – could acquire money in advance in order to grow their crops.

Fig. 19. Salam System.

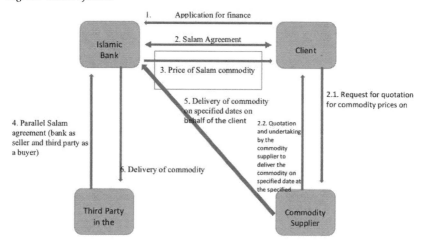

Waqf (Type of Donation/Trust Fund):
Waqf is a financial or non-financial charitable institution refers to a voluntary dedication of one's wealth and property for religious purposes. The waqf property can neither be sold nor inherited or donated to anyone but used for Shariah compliant projects. There are different types of waqf but cash-waqf is one of

the popular type because of its flexibility which allows distribution of the waqf's potential benefit to the poor anywhere. Cash-waqf is expected to become one of the alternative instruments for the poverty alleviation programs in worldwide particularly in Islamic countries. In the Islamic finance system, there is a source of social fund that is economically and politically free of charge, namely cash-waqf that, fund manager collects the fund from waqif and invest the money in the real sector, mainly small and medium-sized ventures and in any Shariah-based investment opportunities. When fund manager takes returns from this investment, then he should allocate the funds to the poverty alleviation program to enhance the quality of poor people's life. He is obliged to maintain the amount of fund in such a way that does not go below the initial amount. This kind of a micro-financing program is considered as the most vital portfolio in the poverty alleviation program.

Istisna (Construction Financing):

Istisna is a forward financing transaction like Salam. It is the other one of the two exceptions to the rules regarding the existence and possession of a commodity prior to entering a contract to sell it. In Istisna pre-delivery financing and leasing structure is used for financing long-term projects and large-scale facilities, such as the construction of refineries, railroads, or bridges. Istisna can be accepted as Islamic type of "Buy, Operate, and Transfer" agreement that the builder accepts the right to operate the highway and collects tolls for a specified period as payment for construction.

4.3 Issues in Interest-Free (Islamic) Financial System Related With Financing Terrorism

Islam is a Holy religion that came to the world in the year 578. It is the second largest religion after Christianity that there are nearly two billion Muslims in the world. In Islam, The Qur'an is the holy book, and Prophet Mohammed his last messenger for people. Mohammed's words and deeds are called Sunnah; both are the fundamental sources of Islamic law, known as Shari'a. Islam has five main pillars. They are Shahabad (profession of faith), Salat (prayer), Zakat (giving of alms), Sawm Ramadan (fasting during the month of Ramadan), and Hajj (pilgrimage to Mecca for those who are able physically and financially). As it was mentioned above, because of the interest is forbidden in Islam, Islamic finance system use the understanding of profit. In other words, it is a kind of financial system which based on especially trade partnership and also appropriate for Islamic rules.

One of the five prominent rules of Islam is Zakat which means in Arabic growth, increase, praise, and cleansing. As a religious term Zakat means, certain assets which must be consumed in certain places if certain conditions occur. If certain conditions occur in Islamic religion, it is an obligation (a religious duty required of all Muslims) that zakat is given. Zakat has an important role in socio-economic life. By the help of zakat, the economic assets of the wealthy are transferred to the poor for unrequitedly. Zakat is commonly referred to as tax or donation. However, Zakat is a holy task for Muslims and there are many differences from taxation system. For example, while zakat is mandatory for all Muslims, taxes are imperative for all economic units or when the zakat is paid directly once a year, the taxes is paid directly or indirectly at various periods. Also, while the ratio of the amount of zakat is fixed, the rate of taxation varies according to the government's fiscal policies. Most importantly, while taxes are paid to the state, zakat is given to certain groups of people who needs. According to Qur'an (Tevbe verse; 60) Zakat is given to poor people, to slaves, to borrowers, to new Muslim people whose hearts could be warmed to Islam, to people who are working for in the name of Allah (it is not fighting for jihad, it includes working for Islam in moral meaning), and to people who are in charge of collecting Zakat (Ozturk, 2017).

According to the scope of zakat obligations is mainly for individuals, but also for companies with legal personality if certain conditions have occurred. Interest-free financial institutions can also be considered in this context. In other words, Zakat is an individual worship. However, the business partners can be in charge of Zakat also. The reason is that the business is considered as a separate legal personality and therefore its assets should be treated as a whole. It is also very clear that interest-free financial institutions will be considered within the scope of the judicial personality, and therefore, they will be evaluated over the whole of their assets while being subjected to Zakat. Because it is not a high authority to calculate zakat rates for the entire Muslim world, interest-free financial institutions have to do their own calculations of zakat. Generally, the amount of zakat for gold, silver, money, and commodities is taken as 2.5% based on the hijri calendar (AAOIFI, 2017; Yatbaz, 2015).

Where does financing terrorism stand in this financial system? This system has not been established for the financing of terrorism. This system is only intended to serve depositors who want to save money in accordance with religious rules. But the absence of authority in Islamic countries, the arbitrary control of non-democratic or Shari'a governments, led to the system becoming out of control.

There is an abuse of Islamic financial institutions because these institutions are governed by Shari'a law and this process is totally different from the process of conventional banking system and its control system. The Islamic financial institutions and banks are obliged to have a control by the Shari'a Committee that has wide-ranging power over all types of the activities of financial institution or bank. This committee, which members are generally well educated Islamic clerics, takes the decisions about which financial tools are appropriate for that institution according to Sharia law. The most important task of the committee is to decide on the amount of zakat and where this amount should go. Generally, the customers have no idea about these decisions of Committee. Islamic banks themselves may not be conspiratorial financiers of terrorism. In most cases, there is nothing illegal in the transactions (Prasad, 2016). Islamic financial institutions or banks use the Zakat funds for charitable purposes. As mentioned above, according to Islamic religion, it is necessary to give Zakat for legal entities. In today's context, these funds are transferred to competent persons who has a right to collect and distribute Zakat or to charity organization, according to the Qur'an. In sometimes these funds that are gathered under the roof of these charities, are being sent to people who need it, but sometimes they are transferred to terrorist organizations. This method is actually one of the simplest methods that can be used in terms of financing terrorism.

It is possible to give more than one example of financing terrorism through Islamic financial institutions. Islamic Bank Bangladesh Limited (hereinafter IBBL) is one of the famous examples that bank transferred their Zakat funds directly to jihadist terrorist groups. In 2011, according to the Bangladeshi home ministry intelligence, 8% of the bank's profits were diverted as corporate zakat to support jihad in Bangladesh (Money Jihad, 2013). If we look back a little longer, the Bank of Credit and Commerce International (hereinafter BCCI) scandal that emerged in 1991 is an important example of terrorist financing and criminal money laundering. Although the BCCI scandal had a different claim, it is known that the bank had been involved in the financing of terrorism. The bank was founded in 1972 by Hasan Abedi from Pakistan, in the Cayman Islands and Luxembourg that was two countries with easiest banking oversight in the world at the time. BCCI played a major role in financing the mujahidin fight against the Soviets in Afghanistan and by opening accounts in the names of charities, NGOs, and businesses controlled by Al-Qaeda. The funds was transferred to Al-Qaeda cells, especially through Pakistani branches, 2 billion dollars of money were flown to Afghan mujahedin. When the bank was closed in July 1991, it had branches in more than 70 countries (Kılıç, 2011; Prasad, 2016)

However, it is not just these two examples. It is possible to find similar examples in many interest-free financial institutions, especially those originating from the Middle East, without a functioning auditing system. The Saudi Islamic financial institution Al Rajhi Bank co-founder Sulaiman Al-Rajhi appeared on the infamous Golden Chain document of Al-Qaeda financiers (Simpson, 2007) and Osama Bin Laden was one of the co-founders of the Al Shamal Islamic Bank in Sudan and invested millions there and after the 1990s Al-Qaeda distributed money that were used in preparation for terrorist attacks, to its cells through Al-Shamal (Brisard, 2002). Several Islamic banks had supported financing terrorist groups. The western world had begun to focus on Islamic financial institutions after September 11. The reason is that after the September 11 attacks, the emergence of the relations of these institutions both with Osama bin Laden other religious extremist groups besides Al-Qaeda. Al-Qaeda was one of the other important examples of terrorist organizations that had abused the Islamic banking system not only by Zakat funds, but also by using other transactions.

4.4 Zakat – Between Religion and Terrorism (Example of Saudi Arabia)

Calling on the Qur'an, Zakat is one of the five duties of Islam. The basic obligation of every Muslim is to separate 2.5% of annual income in goods or money to the poor Muslim population.[16] By giving Zakat, the pleasure and mercy of Allah is attained and the Islamic community is assisted.[17] Since the 1960s with the royal decree, the Zakat is binding on all companies whose owners are residents of Saudi Arabia, as well as all residents in this country. The value of the Zakat that each citizen should give is calculated on the basis of capital gains or income from all means, including income from industry, private business, financial transactions, dividends, and so on. Based on the available data, the Saudi Ministry of Finance annually collects around ten billion US dollars in this way. The legal framework, as well as the strict control of these donor funds in certain countries, contribute to abuse, and corruption in the system by eminent Islamic preachers. Especially those that are influenced by religious movements and teachings. There is a possibility that these funds will be re-used to finance terrorist activities.

In fact the real problem is not the Islamic or interest-free finance institutions. The problem is that these institutions operating within the Islamic laws could

---

16 "believers, separate from the beautiful things that you acquire and from what we give you from the country, do not separate what is not worth to give when you yourself would not take it, except with your eyes closed. And know that Allah is not dependent on anyone, and worthy of gratitude." More see Kuran – Al – Baqarah 2, v. 267;.

17 "The sacred belongs only to the poor and the afflicted, to those who gather it, and to those whose hearts are to be won, and to ransom from slavery and reprobates, for the purpose of Allah's path and for the traveler. Allah has thus decreed – Allah is known and wise." See more Kuran, Surah Taubah 9, v. 60.

not be followed and supervised. Particularly, the money that is collected under the name zakat and which is provided for the purpose of helping different places should be followed up. Because, in the Qur'an, it is determined who will be given the zakat by whom. However, these proposals remain relative to the present world conditions. In addition, although AAOIFI has set a standard for both zakat and other financial transactions, this standard is not binding to all interest-free financial institutions. In this case, these institutions could easily turn into the institutions that provide financing terrorism. Because these institutions usually transfer zakat funds to Islamic charities. However, some Islamic charities financing terrorism or terrorist organization directly. Some of these charities were disclosed but some of them are still undercover. The interest-free financial Institution could transfer their Zakat funds to these charities knowingly or unknowingly. Also, according to the Qur'an, the Zakat funds could be given the people/institution who have right to distribute these funds. In this context, the most important thing for preventing of financing terrorism is closely monitoring the accounting system of these Islamic financial institutions. While the relations between Islamic financial institutions with the financing terrorist organizations are so obvious, much more serious regulation needs to be done in this regard. However, on the other hand, the fact that for only making much more profit, big banks open the new branches with the interest-free banking methods shows that what kind of vicious circle we are in.

5. The Cyber Threat to the Banking Sector

Continued efforts to introduce globalization and liberalization accompanied by the development of technology and the emergence of the Internet have created tectonic shifts' in the functioning of society. The emergence of global interconnected networks and information systems, which made a transformation in the behavior of citizens, businesses, and governments, has created a platform of mutual dependence. With the emergence of the process of globalization a directly proportional process was created, which has benefits for everyone. For the ordinary man a boon, for criminals an open space for unlimited projection of their possibilities, and no one can assume where the limit is.

Changes in the economic and technological development on a global level have reflected the changes in the profile, shape, and method of operation of financial institutions and their organizations. Generally speaking, the changes are related to:

1. **Liberalization of banking operations** – enables deregulation of banking operations on the domestic and the foreign market or removing of financial barriers, allowing flexible operations and more competitiveness internationally (Haselmann & Vig, 2007).
2. **Development of information technology** – provides flexibility of the banks, satisfies the needs of their customers through introduction and placement of new products [electronic banking (e-banking)] (Aliyu & Tasmin, 2012).
3. **Globalization of the international market** (Levitt, 1983) – liberalization of the banking operations at the national level and the accelerated growth needs for the banking services on an international level has enabled the strengthening and interdependence of banks.

Precisely, the introduction and distribution of new products into the banking system is an open field in which the perpetrators of crimes found a solution to commit criminal activities and abuse.

The increase in cyberattacks, especially in the financial information infrastructure as a vital segment of each nation, whereby damage is done directly to the customer, and then to the bank's reputation, threatening the circulation of financial transactions and causing a handicap to the economy, has become a challenge for all countries so that they are giving priority to the national defense and security doctrines/strategies.

In order to prevent such attacks or similar critical infrastructure, whether it be a physical or a cyberattack, every country should have a strategic plan for the prevention, rapid response and rapid removal of the consequences and return to the normal workflow of the attacked infrastructure. The plan should include:

– An assessment of weaknesses that could lead to a physical or cyberattack;
– A plan for the removal of significant weaknesses;
– Developing systems to identify and prevent attempts to attack;
– Signaling of a possible attack and attack resistance;
– Renewal of the working capacity of the attacked system.

Although, the major part of the financial critical infrastructure is controlled by the industrial control systems also known as Supervisory Control and Data Acquisition (SCADA), or other programs that are vulnerable to hackers and distributed denial-of-services (hereinafter DDoS) attacks, an easier way to enter into the banking information system is to attack the users, in this case, the customers which used e-services of the bank or e-banking.

5.1 Overview of E-Banking Services

"Distribution of banking services and products includes: bank deposits and loans, accounting management, as well as the provision of other products and services (e.g., E-cash) for electronic payment" is the definition of the term e-banking given by the Committee on Banking Supervision (Basel Committee for Banking Supervision, 2000). In expert circles there is no universal definition of e-banking, because it encompasses a variety of services that could be realized in different shapes using different devices. According to Georgieva – Trajkova, e-banking is an "automatic delivery of new and traditional banking products directly to consumers through electronic, interactive communication channels" (Georgieva-Trajkovska, 2009). Also, Federal Financial Institution Examination Council defined e-banking "as the automated delivery of new and traditional banking products and services directly to customers through electronic, interactive communication channels" (Federal Financial Institution Examination Council, 2003).

E-banking enables customers to use modern electronic devices (PC, ATM, EFT POS – Electronic Fund Transfer at Point-of-Sale, etc.), direct access to their accounts, realization of transactions or direct access to information on financial products and services through a public or private network, including the Internet. Here, it is important to make a difference between the concepts of e-banking and online banking, according to which the concept of e-banking is broader and covers more ways of realizing the banking services through electronic devices that are not based on Internet technology. These include home banking which can be performed via a telephone line, intranet, Internet, and so far, the most sophisticated channel, the mobile phone. Through this option, the customer can, from his home, house or area beyond the bank premises establish a link with the bank's computer center. Depending on the stage of development the home banking link between the client and the computer system of the bank can be established through a phone, TV, or computer. Based on the method of establishment of the link, we distinguish:

– Phone banking
– Intranet banking
– Internet banking

5.1.1 Phone Banking

Telephone banking is a service offered by the bank through which customers have the opportunity to realize banking transactions over the phone or get information via the voice machine [interactive voice response (hereinafter IVR)].

Depending on the way a link between the client and the bank is established, these services can be realized in two ways:

–   The operator of the Bank
–   Computer Center of the Bank

According to the first method, the customer establishes a telephone contact with the operator and gives further instructions for the implementation of certain services (account balance and payment cards, the number of appropriations, a description of products and services of the bank, etc.).

The second method requires special conditions under which the client should have a phone with a special reader data on a magnetic tape, or a special keyboard through which the client enters the username and password. Upon validation, the client has access to entry into the banking system, which allows access to the banking services. To enter the username and password, the clients frequently use a token: hardware or software. When the user wants to use banking services he receives a single-use security code through a token.

Risks that could occur when using telephone banking are:

–   Unauthorized wiretapping using special equipment for wiretapping and thus to obtain the personal data of the user data on the number of bank account numbers of credit cards, etc. through which abuse and unlawful acquisition of unlawful proceeds can be performed.
–   Attack of the token with a harmful virus that can be software and, in that way, provide data about the client, bank account numbers, credit card numbers, and so on. There is a possibility of intrusion into the computer system of the bank in order to gain access to customer data, the numbers of their accounts, and so on.

5.1.2 Online Banking

Online banking allows execution of banking transactions via direct computer connection between the client and the bank using a special software program that should be installed on the client's computer or user. Besides the software, due to double security, the user is required to possess a special smart card reader and a smart card on which a digital certificate is inscribed. The reader should be connected to the computer. In order for the client to gain access to the program, it is necessary to insert a smart card into the reader and insert the password. The connection between the user and the banking system is accomplished when the digital certificate of the smart card is activated. Communication is done via a closed network communication system of the bank (INTRANET), through the use of a modem.

This type of banking is often used by legal entities due to the static on the computer, special software installed and expensive training.

As a potential risk of using online banking, the following can be distinguished:

- Unauthorized intrusion into the user's computer through the use of harmful malware software in order to get his personal information, bank account numbers, and so on.

5.1.3 Internet Banking

Internet banking is the realization of bank transactions and accesses and collection of information by using the Internet service.

The principle is based on the use of the World Wide Web. Through the browser the client has direct access and has the ability to pay bills, insight into the account balance, the transfers realized, etc.

Internet banking has many advantages, and includes the following: saving time, the opportunity to perform work from home or any computer, lower costs and commissions, 24-hour availability, realization of high-speed transactions, and confidentiality of data.

However, Internet banking also has drawbacks: the possibility of abuse by fishing attacks, harmful viruses' malware, Trojan, etc.

5.1.4 Mobile Banking [Wireless Application Protocol (WAP) Banking]

The development of technology has led to the sophistication of the relationship between the customer and the bank. The emergence of portable computers (Laptop, Notebook, and Tablet) and cellular smartphones pervades the issue which many experts bring to the table; the question is, where is the limit, or where does this process end? Will the kitchens of innovative technological companies offer more sophisticated devices that would improve the relationship customer – bank? These products have enabled the use of banking services 24/7 a week, from any place on the planet that is covered by a Global System for Mobile communication (GSM) signal. Benefits provided by mobile banking are: payment movement, transfer of funds from an account to an account, checking of account balance, paying bills for electricity, water, etc.

The communication between the client and the bank can be realized in two ways: through SMS messages and via a WAP application. Android wireless application protocol (hereinafter AWAP) application is a separate software program that is installed on the mobile device and by connecting to the Internet via a cellular provider. The users perform a direct connection to the banking system, whereby they can give instructions for further activities.

In order to increase the safety and normal functioning of the current process, banks have developed applications through which customers have easier access to services. In order to access the service, the client must identify and then enter the security code. Auditing of the identity of the client and its authorization is contrary to the traditional procedure, where the client must be identified by an identification document (ID or passport); the banks offered alternative methods to verify the authenticity of data through:

- PIN code – Personal identification number
- Public key infrastructure (hereinafter PKI) – Digital certificate
- Token
- Database comparators
- Biometric identifiers

5.1.5 New Forms of Distribution of Banking Services

Automated Teller Machines – ATM
ATM devices or popularly called ATMs are automated devices through which the customer has access to certain banking services. How do they work? ATMs are directly related to their "host" or ATM controller via an asymmetric digital subscriber line Asymmetric digital subscriber line (ADSL) link or a dial-up modem. Through the ATM, the customer has a 24-hour access to his account and a wide range of services: deposit and cash withdrawal, transfer from an account to an account, paying of bills, information on exchange rates, account balance, and etc.

Prestige and race in the creation of its own network of ATMs has led to increased costs for the banks. For this reason and in order to reduce costs, based on mutual agreement, the banks have started creating an integrated model of the ATM network through which the client can use the services of ATMs of other banks via a payment card from a bank.

POS terminal (Point-of-Sale – POS)
Prestige and race to attract more clients enable companies to offer financial services through which customers can buy goods or pay with electronic money via a credit card or a smartphone. On the other hand, this payment system is a protective mechanism by which the owner of the company itself is protected from abuse by its employees.

The modern POS system is an electronic communication system through which the link between the customer, the bank, and the trader is established. POS terminals are directly connected to the computer network of the bank and the client through the terminal provides the electronic order to the bank that the funds from his account be transferred to the account of the retail trader.

5.2 Determined Risks Due to the Use of E-Banking Services

All financial institutions that offer e-banking services to its customers in parallel must assess potential risks that may occur and thereby provide procedures that will protect their customers, their personal data, and to ensure security and authenticity of transactions. The most common risks that a financial institution which offers e-banking services and users of e-banking services in the country may face are:

- Internet fraud
- Harmful software
- Misuse of payment cards
- DDoS attacks on information infrastructure

The abovementioned actions represent the predicate offenses in which the offender may acquire illegal profit. In order to conceal the source of illegal properties (usually in the form of cash), the perpetrator puts the cash into the financial system and pursues a process of money laundering. Here, we come to the purpose of this research, to determine what the possible risks from abusing e-banking with the aim to acquire illegal proceeds are and their integration into the financial system, which constitutes an act of money laundering.

5.2.1 Internet Fraud

5.2.1.1 Identity Theft

Identity theft is a crime under which the perpetrator uses or abuses the identity of another person without their knowledge and approval. For this purpose, the perpetrator of an unlawful act accesses the personal data of the victim (identity card, passport, identification number, PIN code access security clearance, and so on).

Identity theft is realized in three different phases:

- Unlawful acquisition of data about the person (classical theft of personal documents and identification documents) through unauthorized access to their computer system via Trojans, "key-login" spyware and other malware, or through phishing and other social engineering techniques.

- Possession and use of personal data. This includes the sale of such data through underground economy, which offers data on credit card numbers, bank accounts, passwords, and so on.
- Use of personal data in order to perform fraud and other crimes (opening of bank accounts, applying for loans, transfers of funds, orders of goods, etc.) through which fraudsters unlawfully acquire material benefit.

5.2.1.2 Identity Fraud and Social Engineering

Fraud by abuse of identity is a criminal offense under which the perpetrator engages in unauthorized use of the data of the victim in order to unlawfully acquire goods, services, and financial assets. In this case, we have two predicate crimes in which the offender may acquire illegal profit. Thus, the offender might misuse the personal data of the victim with electronic access to e-banking and thus electronically submit a credit application on behalf of the victim, to access and dispose of his account, transfer funds from the account of the victim to other accounts without their knowledge, and so on. The offender thus acquires assets that may be used for money laundering in order to move away from the source and hide this tracks.

Social engineering involves consciously manipulating the person (victim) on the part of the offender in order to acquire certain data in an unauthorized way, or to force the victim to perform a particular activity. Previously, we mentioned that a much easier way to perform penetration into the banking information system is indirectly through customers rather than directly.

In this case, the perpetrator does not make attempts to identify, trace, and exploit any weaknesses in security controls of the banking information system and perform penetration through relevant and sophisticated tools and application hacking techniques. He tries to get to the client (the victim), to create a sense of confidence, so that the victim gets a sense of misconception about the true identity of the perpetrator. The goal is to acquire personal data of the victim, his bank account numbers, credit card numbers, passwords, and security codes, PINs, access to security certificates, etc., and, thus, the perpetrator will gain illegal profit.

In such cases, the perpetrator is usually identified via his fake identity as the victim's acquaintance, his co-worker, relative, business partner, as the one falsifying the e-mail address of the sender and abusing the protective logos of companies, and so on.

5.2.1.3 Mass-Marketing Fraud-Phishing

Mass – marketing fraud – most used schemes with mass-marketing fraud – are schemes which target large numbers of victims for small financial losses on an individual basis, and schemes which target large amounts of people for significantly higher wage amounts. Both schemes are financially damaging, and both of them require immediate attention. Mass-fraud refers to the method in which a person defrauds a large number of people. Many of these criminals sent e-mails to "phish" for victims. Phishing is a major social engineering technique that is used as a tool for stealing data about persons or fraud. It most often occurs in the form of spear phishing (invented messages aimed at a specific person), "pharming" (redirect traffic from legitimate sites to fake sites' illegitimate users in order to provide their data), and "smishing" SMS to which asks for data. These e-mails often ask the clients to download an attachment, which contains a computer virus. Other e-mails might request personal information in exchange for financial payment. They operate under the guise of a legitimate business, and people who are not naturally skeptical often become victims. Internet, mail, and telemarketing fraud are all primary ways in which people fall victim to these types of criminals.

Here is an example of what a phishing scam in an e-mail message might look like:

Example 1: Customer receive e-mail
Dear customer!
In order to continue our cooperation, we would like to offer you a new collection for the summer of 2017.
On the following link, you can find our new catalog for 2017:
https://brendstore.com/catalog2017
Regards
Brendstore team!
How it looks in practice:

This scam is designed to collect sensitive data about the user often digitally punctuated for personal identification (usernames and passwords, PINs for payment cards, PIN-ROMs for access to a digital certificate, etc.). For this purpose, the perpetrator disguises or uses a fake profile or data from a third person or company with the sole purpose to resemble an entity of trust in electronic communication in which the user has already established cooperation.

Fraud over phone calls Usually such scams, criminals make posing as bank employees offering new products to customers. In telephone conversations, criminals' direct clients to tell their personal data, identification numbers, and data on bank cards, their passwords, etc.

Picture 6. Scam of a Phishing Attack Against a User of e-banking Services.

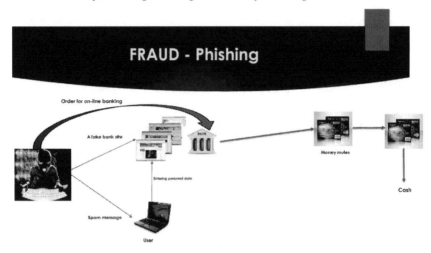

5.2.1.4 Nigerian Fraud

Nigerian scam or the scam known as "419 Fraud" appeared during the 1980s of the last century in Nigeria at a time when the country was experiencing economic growth based on the exploitation of oil resources. Namely, a few students who have not yet established a working relationship used methods of deception to mislead certain business structures that have an interest or want to make an interest in Nigeria through trade with oil and thus secure it for their own purposes. Namely, in the late evening hours in Internet cafes students sent letters or e-mails about business cooperation from certain companies in Nigeria. These messages were designed to look like they were deliberately sent to users. The fraud starts by convincing "victims" to participate in the distribution of a cash fund if paid a certain amount of money in advance, or mediation to open a business in Nigeria, and so on. This phenomenon over time developed in other parts of the world and is today mostly done by sending SPAM messages to "potential victims" which requires a certain amount of money for "Help", "Participation in the lottery", etc.

5.2.2 Harmful Software (Malware)

Malware is a software that is fed into the information system in order to do harm to the system or other systems to obstruct their functioning, to receive information or to seduce systems and customized use that users are not even aware of. Commonly used malware includes viruses, computer worms, and Trojans that enter through the security protection on your computer, import additional malware or infected files or stolen data, and personal data about the user used by using e-banking. Some malware programs can be disguised to look like legitimate software. In order to create confusion among the user, malware attacks usually come from an official website of a known company, bank, etc., in the form of a useful or attractive program that is rooted Malware with special software that is tasked to collect data from the user's computer.

Picture 7. Scam of Malicious Software "Malware".

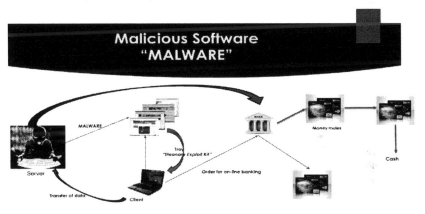

5.2.2.1 Intercepted Communication

One of the most dangerous risks for online banking services is interception of communication. The criminals use malware to capture communication between the client and online banking officer. When communication is intercepted, all details for account, money transferring process, and payment process are transmitted to the criminals' computer server. Then, criminals exploit the compromised account and transferring funds into the mule account or use data for applying credit/debit cards in the customer name or other things.

Picture 8. Scam of Interception of Communication.

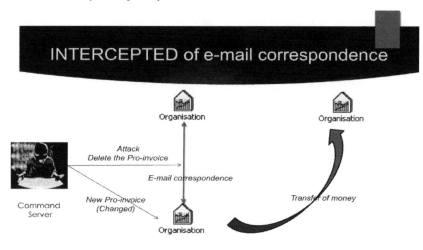

5.2.3 Payment Card Fraud

Fraud with payment cards is mostly committed through perpetrating crimes, including:

- Skimming/Cloning – interception of card details (Skimming) that can be sold or used to make a duplicate credit card (cloning). The process of intercepting data is usually executed on ATMs where "Skimmers" are placed or at POS terminals at retail points ("Mobile Skimmers"). Stolen data is used to make counterfeit credit cards or sold on the internet (underground economy).
  - ➢ Skimmers are special devices through which perpetrators of data collect in an unlawful manner data inscribed on the magnetic strip of the payment card and PIN code. These devices can be: (1) fixed and usually placed on ATMs and (2) mobiles that read the record from the magnetic strip.

Credit card fraud comes in many different shapes and forms, including fraud that involves using a payment card of some description, and more. There are two main reasons for credit card fraud. One is that criminals are designed to obtain funds from accounts, while others wish to obtain goods for free. Furthermore, it is very important to understand that credit card fraud is linked closely to identity theft. Michael Bennett, expert and editor-in-Chief of Consumer Protect.com, in 2015 explains that "credit card fraud is not just single action". According to him, 11 forms of credit card fraud existing on the field. They are following:

- Application Fraud
- Electronic or Manual Credit Card Imprints
- CNP (Card Not Present) Fraud
- Counterfeit Card Fraud
- Lost or stolen Card Fraud
- Card ID Theft
- Mail Non-Receipt Card Fraud
- Assumed Identity
- Doctored Cards
- Fake Cards and
- Account Takeover. (Bennet, 2015)

Before, in 2013, Richard Glanville also mentioned the same types of Credit Card Fraud (Glanville, 2013). Also, Council of Europe Committee of Experts on the Evaluation of Anti-Money Laundering Measures and the Financing of Terrorism (hereinafter MONEYVAL) Committee in his Research Report "Criminal money flows on the internet: methods, rends, and multi-stakeholder counteraction" mentioned several types of payment card fraud which are the same with above-mentioned (MONEYVAL COMMITTEE – Council of Europe, 2012).

How thieves steal credit card information and generate illegal profits of that. This process can be separated into three main phases. First stage is obtaining information. To do that, the thief use physical attack, insider attack, and attack from outside which means illegal access to computer system, spyware and other malware, or phishing attack and through using of other social engineering techniques. Also, skimming is one of most often used techniques by criminals to steal data from credit card. They used electronic devices to copy and store credit card information. Very often used technique is phishing. It is a scam to get personal information like ID numbers, passwords, usernames, account number or card numbers from consumers occur via e-mail, phone or text or snail mail. Through spyware thieves collect credit card information without knowledge or consent. This special software is designing to collect credit card and banking information as well as user logins from computers it's installed on. In this case, thieves attack an object which means computers of consumers or servers of banking institutions or other private companies. The possession and disposal of information is second stage. When thieves have information about data of credit cards they can make sale in the e-underground economy or on black market and gain money for that. And finally, third stage is use of credit cards or credit cards data. In first situation, thieves used credit cards to online to purchase items which are typically reshipped by mules operating in various areas. On second situation, credit cards data can be used to duplicate cards (cloned) and to withdraw money from ATM machines or paying of items.

5.2.4 Distributed Dental of Attack on the Work of the Banking Information System (DDoS Attacks)

The efficient system of corporate security protects the system from possible aggressive actions. It allows the formation of a platform for making important management decisions at the bank related to the introduction of new products, the establishment of cooperation with businesses, providing confidential information to the management and prevention of leakage of confidential information from the bank.

DDoS attack means preventing access to the computer system or network resource temporarily in order to make them unavailable for users. The most common methods of DDoS attacks include saturation of the target device with external communication requests to the extent that the device is unable to competently respond to legitimate requests or responds so slowly that it essentially becomes too slow. These attacks led to overloading of the server.

5.2.4.1 Attacks on the Banks

There is a clear consensus that digital currencies pose a ML/TF threat. A small number of cases have already shown Law Enforcement Agencies that ML/TF can easily take place inside virtual environments, offering high levels of anonymity and low levels of detection removing many of the risks associated with real-world ML/TF activities.

From other side introduction and distribution of new products into the banking system is an open field in which the perpetrators of crimes found a solution to commit criminal activities and abuse. The most common risks that a financial institution which offers e-banking services and users of e-banking services are Internet fraud, harmful software, APT – Advanced Persistent Threat, payment cards fraud, and DDoS attacks on critical financial information infrastructure. These actions represent the predicate offenses in which the offender may acquire illegal profit. In order to conceal the source of illegal properties (usually in the form of cash), the perpetrator puts the cash into the financial system and pursues a process of money laundering.

Comparing the main motivation for cybercrime in last 2 years, during 2016, percentage of events motivated by cybercrime raised from 67% to 72,1%, while hacktivism dropped to 14,2% from 20,8%. Cyber Espionage was essentially stable, from 9,8% to 9,2% in 2016, whereas Cyber Warfare has nearly doubled, from 2,4% in 2015 to 4,3% in 2016 (Passeri, 2017).

Picture 9. Motivations Behind Attacks: 2015 vs 2016.

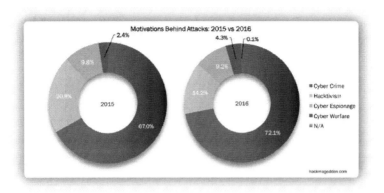

Source: Passeri (2017).

According to the abovementioned, money is the main motivation for cybercrime. Banks as a major source of funds and data are the main targets and challenges for criminals. For cybercriminals, banks represent a high risk/reward proposition. Banks tend to have a great deal of investment in cyber-protection – more so following a few of the most recent attacks mentioned before – but on the other hand, the information they contain is easily converted into cash. Some of the information literally *is* cash, which can be grabbed from compromised bank accounts and drained into the coffers of off-shore tax havens and unfriendly nations. Other client information's – addresses, phone numbers, e-mails, bank statements, number of banks accounts, PIN codes, and social security numbers (hereinafter SSNs) – also can be sold into the hands of eager scammers, or on black markets and dark webs.

In spite of recent heavy investment by banks into cybersecurity, there have still been times when a bank's information security defenses have acted less like an iron vault, and more like a piñata. Some of the most devastating cyberattacks on banks in the history of cybersecurity show that main motivation of cyber criminals is money. In case called "CARBANAK", a multinational gang of cybercriminals infiltrated with APT network attack in more than 100 banks across 30 countries and made off with up to one billion dollars over a period of roughly 2 years. The characteristics of CARBANAK case are the following:

- Objects of attack: Financial institutions (more than 100 banks);
- Geographical areas: Internationally (USA, Russia, China, Germany, Ukraine);
- Technique of attack: Spear Phishing
- Points of attack: System administrators
- Damage: Approximately 1 Billion US Dollars.

APT is a network attack in which an unauthorized person gains access to a network and stays hidden and undetected for a long period. The main intention of APT is to be monitoring the network and/or stealing data rather than to cause damage to the network or financial organization.

One of the largest breaches in history is JP Morgan Data Breach. It was happened in 2014 and affected tens of millions of people, and several million businesses. Gang group used malware, social engineering, and spear – phishing attacks to plunder personal information of customers. The damage was $100 million before being shut down.

Other biggest attack happened in Bangladesh in 2016. A Bangladeshi central bank official's computer was used by unidentified hackers to make payments via society for worldwide interbank financial telecommunication (hereinafter SWIFT) and carry out one of the biggest-ever cyber heists. The hackers sent fraudulent messages, ostensibly from the central bank in Dhaka, on the SWIFT system, to the New York Federal Reserve seeking to transfer nearly $1 billion from Bangladesh Bank's account there. Most of the transfers were blocked but about $81 million was sent to a bank in the Philippines. It was moved to casinos and casino agents and much of it is missing.

Shortly after that incident, Russian central bank officials disclosed that hackers stole more than $31 million (two billion rubles) from the country's central bank and commercial banks.

In DDoS scenario, hackers take over multiple computers remotely, send continuous requests to overwhelm the targeted server and deny it the ability to fulfill its duty to providing news stories, banking services, or video-streaming in Turkey in December 2015. More than 400,000 websites registered under Turkey's Internet domain "tr." were attacked and experienced problems.

5.3 Protection of the Bank Information Infrastructure

With the purpose to minimize the risk of loss for the bank arising from losing, unauthorized utilization, or unavailability of the information, information services, the banks shall be obligated to establish a system for early identification, measurement, monitoring, and control of the information system incompatibility risk.[18]

The security of the banks' information system is conditioned with the fulfillment of three basic criteria:

---

18 Decision on the bank's information system security is adopted by National Assembly of the Republic of Macedonia ("Official Gazette of the Republic of Macedonia" No. 31/2008).

- **Confidentialty** – availability of the information system for users who have authorized access to it;
- **Integrity** – Safeguarding of the accuracy and completeness of the information system;
- **Availability** – Security of unrestricted access to the banks' information system for the authorized users.

Along the abovementioned criteria for a secure bank information system, the banks should undertake additional activities with the main aim to protect the system for e-banking. For this purpose, the banks should secure the following security criteria:

- **Confirmation of the identity of the client**: a system for unique identification verification and authentication of the information system users' identity shall be applied through the following methods:
  - *Through a set of symbols (PIN code, password, etc.)*
  - *Through an Electronic card, token, etc.*
  - *Through recognition of personal physical features of the client (fingerprint, iris, speech recognition, etc.)*
- **Transaction non-repudiation**: a system for verification of the information integrity and providing of evidence for the transfer of certain information or transaction performed by a certain user through confirmation of his identity with a combination of at least two of the abovementioned defined methods.

Along with protecting the system for e-banking, the bank shall be obligated to lead and implement the Information System Security Policy, defining the foundations for the process of managing the information system security risks. This Policy includes:

- Protection of personal data of their clients in accordance with the laws;
- Classifying both information and information assets in the bank;
- Management of security incidents and establishment of a suitable mechanism for their identification, reporting and efficient elimination of the possible threats to the information security system;
- Risks assessment and their categorization;
- Procedure of establishing anti-virus protection;
- Procedure for defining the manner of telecommunication connection and ensuring protection to the data to be transferred;
- Defining security zones in the bank and restricting the physical access to the bank's information and information assets, etc.

6. Money Transfer Methods for Terrorism Financing

The movement of funds from the source to the terrorist organization is a very important process, due to the fact that it should remain undetected by the prosecuting authorities. The method of money transfer will depend on many factors. However, in general, there are three basic methods that terrorists use to transfer money or high value goods from the source to the terrorist organization:

1. Using the financial system
2. Physical transport of money or high value goods (courier system) and
3. Using an informal system for transferring funds.

Also, terrorist organizations abuse non-profit organizations or other entities in order to conceal the three methods of transferring funds. The most frequently mentioned alternative method, and according to research the most inconspicuous, is the so-called "Hawala" money transfer system. All of these methods will be thoroughly explained later in the book.

Globalization, the advancement of technology, and the large organizational structure of terrorist organizations hinder the detection of the most commonly used method for transferring money. If terrorists were once thought to be psychopaths, sick people, today we have a situation where terrorist organizations are led by highly educated individuals who often use expert opinions and advice on how to organize and lead the terrorist organization until the realization of its ultimate goal. Whereas the perpetrators of terrorist acts can be mentally disordered persons and individuals under the influence of narcotic drugs or other opiates, etc.

Knowing the legislation and systems for controlling and monitoring the transfer of funds by the competent authorities, terrorists often use false identities to open bank accounts through which they transfer money or use accounts of fictitious organizations or firms so that the authorities cannot detect the transfer of funds.

Such a range of methods for transferring funds by terrorist organizations rightfully leads us to think and conclude that terrorists use all possible methods for transferring funds from the source to the organization.

This represents an added difficulty in the detection and differentiation between daily financial activities and funds used for financing terrorist activities.

Identification and prevention of terrorism financing is difficult even when the competent authorities are faced with "informal" support networks that do not function as part of a well-structured organization with clear roles and responsibilities.

Experience shows that all the mechanisms for transferring funds around the world are risky in every respect, and there is always a possibility and way to be detected and stopped. A common thing for all of them is the difficulty of determining the connection between the money and terrorism in the countries that provide the funds and the place where the terrorist act is carried out if it is located in another country.

6.1 Using the Financial Sector for Transferring Funds for Terrorism Financing

In almost all countries, the financial institutions and other financial service providers (credit bureaus, savings banks, exchange offices, fast money transfer, etc.) are regulated by law. They represent an official financial sector and are used as main instruments through which all types of transactions between legal and natural persons are transferred. The wide range of services and products (loans, credit cards, online banking, ATM's, purchasing by phone, etc.) serve as a means and way through which money is transferred to a terrorist organization. The detection of such transactions is particularly difficult both within the home country and internationally, knowing the speed and simplicity of transferring funds from one place to another.

The problem becomes more difficult if a connection is found between off-shore companies and terrorist organizations, because such countries have a so-called "weak" financial and legal system where control and supervision are of a very low level (UN Security Council, 2002). Such entities provide effective coverage that is necessary for the transfer of transactions, as well as for the realization of the process of laundering money obtained through criminal activities. The purpose of placing money in the banking system and their further processing is always the same, to hide the connection between the client and the end user of the funds. And, a client can be any person who is directly or indirectly connected to the terrorist organization.

Terrorists often use the system of "fast money transfer" that requires less information for identifying the client and end user, further complicating the process and procedure of detecting suspicious transactions related to terrorism financing. They are obliged to identify the persons who send money from one country and the persons who receive the money in another country. In this way a network of cooperation between terrorist organizations and their transfers is established, but also a strong trace is left that would be of great importance in the detection of the whole scheme of financing terrorist organizations by the prosecuting authorities.

New products offered by the banking sector, such as e-banking, further complicate the identification of the client because the account can be opened by a person with a false identity and is used for the transfer of transactions for terrorism financing. Then, the client's identification (the person performing the transaction) is impossible because the bank's knowledge will be that the client is the one who opened the account. However, the person who owns the account can give the password for electronic access to persons who are connected to a terrorist organization or are part of it.

The high speed and large number of money transfers, when there is no constant implementation of the standards proposed by the FATF[19] Special Recommendation VII for determining key information for such transactions, keeping records, and information for the transaction, can serve as a monitoring instrument by the investigating authorities.

6.2 Courier Service for Transferring Cash and High Value Goods

One of the easiest ways to avoid barriers placed by systems for preventing ML/TF within financial systems is to physically transfer funds from the source to the end users using a courier or also known as "money mule." The transfer does not always imply money, but conversion of cash into checks, shares, gold, diamonds, material goods, etc.,[20] which can later be sold and returned in the original form, i.e., money. A large percentage of such cases are done with a calculated risk, i.e.,

---

19 FATF is an inter-governmental body established in 1989 at the G7 Summit in Paris. The purpose of this body is to develop and promote policy (at national and international level) for combating money laundering and terrorist financing. The FATF is a "policy-making body" which works to generate the necessary political will to bring about national legislative and regulatory reforms in these areas. The FATF monitors the progress of its members in implementing necessary measures, reviews money laundering, terrorist financing techniques, and counter-measures for combating these evils. In addition, it collaborates with other international stakeholders involved in the fight against ML/TF. The FATF currently comprises 34 member jurisdictions and 2 regional organizations.

20 While transferring money from the source to the terrorist organization, the financial network for supporting the terrorist organization often converts money (money laundering) into goods (vehicles, branded goods, etc.) This is because these funds are bought on the common market where there is no person identification. In this way, couriers are protected and cannot be identified as suspicious persons by the competent authorities (banks) or by the customs service when they cross the border. Then, these goods are sold in another country for any price (always with a calculated risk) and the money is delivered to the terrorist organization. This way of transferring funds was used by the Moroccan terrorist organization operating in southern Portugal and Spain where it bought high value vehicles and shipped them to North African countries where they were sold. They money was used to fund local Islamist terrorist groups.

the selling price of shares, gold, diamonds, and other goods is always lower than the purchase price.

Previous experience and practice of anti-terrorist operations in the detection of terrorist financing schemes have shown that courier services are mostly used by countries of the Middle East and South Asia for the physical transfer of cash and precious metals. Also, the transfer of cash across borders is more common in countries in which e-banking is in development or the population rarely uses it. In several countries in Africa and the Middle East, the economy is cash-based, which practically means cash flows are transferred by courier services or alternative money transfer systems are used.

The transfer of funds by courier services is more expensive than the electronic transfer of funds. As institutions involved in the system for preventing terrorism financing have strengthened their due diligence measures, this activity for transferring money by couriers became more appealing to terrorist organizations because it leaves no traces by which transactions could be detected. If the transfer of money is detected, then it is very difficult to determine the origin and end use of the funds. During the investigation, the investigating authorities sometimes allow this transfer of funds to be carried out in order to determine the end user, i.e., the end use of the funds.

6.3 Informal Money Transfer System for Terrorism Financing – "Hawala"

This informal value transfer system is based on trust and allows national or international transfer of property, money, and high value goods without leaving any traces.

Hawala (known as "Huwala" in the Gulf States and "Hundi"in India) meaning transfer or sometimes trust is an international financial network that is not regulated by law and is used in order to transfer funds to other persons, relatives, etc., who cannot open an account in a bank or do not want to be identified by financial institutions. In the most basic variant of the hawala system, money is transferred via a network of brokers (the so-called *hawaladars*) (Patrick & Harjit, 2005).

For further information, see: TE – SAT 2008 – EU Terrorism Situation and trends, European Police Office, 2008, p. 23.

Basic features of hawala:

1. **Low cost**
   - *No registration of the business;*
   - *No founding capital;*
   - *No taxes;*
   - *No personnel costs and*
   - *No technical equipment.*
2. **High degree of flexibility**
   - *Sanctions avoidance;*
   - *Non-existent banking system and*
   - *Humanitarian aid.*
3. **Anonymity**
   - *Avoidance of foreign exchange controls;*
   - *Clients are not identified;*
   - *No documentation for the transaction;*
   - *There are no obligations to prove the origin of funds;*
   - *Tax evasion and*
   - *Evasion of customs duties.*

Fig. 20. Informal Value Transfer System "Hawala".

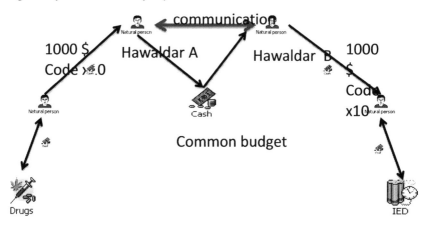

The person M.M. from country X made 2,500 EUR by selling drugs. If this money is placed in the financial system it can be identified, the transaction can be followed to the end user, and if the prosecuting authorities identify suspicious activities, they can take measures and actions to stop the transaction and initiate a procedure for determining the origin of the funds and their end user. In order to avoid that risk, the person M.M. gives the money to the hawaladar from country X under a unique code A10 and gives data on the end user. The hawaladar of country X informs the hawaladar from country Y about the amount of the transaction, the unique code, and the end user. The person M. M. from country X informs the person N. N. from country Y about the amount of the transaction, the funds, the unique code, and the hawaladar from country Y who should release the money in the amount of 2,500EUR. The person N. N. with residence in country Y comes to the hawaladar's country of residence, and with the unique code A10 takes the money from the hawaladar in the total amount of 2,500EUR. For the service rendered by hawaladars, the person M. M. or N. N. pays a certain commission or fee.

The settlement of positions between the hawaladars is done through a common fund. And, if money is transferred to the fund in one country, it is withdrawn from the fund in the other country. The state of the fund is always the same.

There is also a Hundi system that is widespread on the Indian subcontinent, Fei-Ch'ien (China), Padala (Philippines), Hui Kuan (Hong Kong), and Phei Kwan (Thailand) (Qorchi, Maimbo, & Wilson, 2003). As we explained above, the hawala is a kind of an illegal money transfer system, while the hundi can be described as a system for illegal trade and credit transactions.

.

Chapter II. International Response to the Financing of Terrorism

Financing terrorism, which has an international dimension and transboundary nature, is not a danger that only one country can prevent by its own means and endeavors. International organizations have developed measures within the struggle against financing terrorism for guiding the states on this issue and have created special units for this struggle. Meanwhile, the most important point to be emphasized is that terrorism financing is accompanied by the concept of money laundering. In this chapter, measures taken at international level against financing terrorism will be explained in terms of international institutions. In this context, the subject will be addressed within the measures of the UN, the Council of Europe, the EU and the FATF.

1. United Nations

The fight against terrorism is not a new issue for the UN. The UN was aware of the necessity of fighting terrorism from all aspects, in fact before September 11, and in this context, many conventions accomplished by the UN since 1963 in the fight against terrorism. However, the majority of these regulations relate to issues beyond financing terrorism. These conventions, which are issued worldwide, relate to issues such as terrorism, aircraft hijacking, piracy, hostage taking, bombing of civilians, and the acquisition of nuclear materials. These conventions had increased the diplomatic mobility that necessary to combating terrorism, due to offering the intensive cooperation.

One of the major financial sources of terrorism is drug trafficking and its revenues. Although it was not directly targeted to terrorism, in 1988 the *"Convention Against Illicit Traffic in Narcotic Drugs And Psychotropic Substances for the Fight Against Drugs and Money Laundering"* known as the Vienna Convention was accepted. The Vienna Convention has become the cornerstone of the UN efforts to counter the threat posed by narcotics and it has been described as "heart of an effective strategy to counter modern international drug trafficking" (Ryder, 2015). The Convention aimed to increase cooperation between the state parties in order to ensure a more effective fight against drug and psychotropic substance trafficking. Although the text did not directly convey a "money laundering" statement, the Convention is the first UN convention to define it as an element of the criminal offense (UN Convention, 1988).

The scope of the Vienna Convention was narrow and this weakness was rectified by the Palermo Convention, to include the "proceeds of serious crime". The Palermo Convention broadened the scope of the criminalization of drug money laundering to all "serious offences". On the other hand, in 1999, the *United Nations Security Council created a Resolution (UNSCR) 1267* that directed at Al-Qaeda and its supporters in the Taliban regime of Afghanistan. The sanctions committee was formed to oversee and implement the resolution of the individuals and entities subject to financial sanctions and gathering identifying information. As with all sanctions regimes at the time, however, the enforcement of the financial measures was limited (Biersteker & Eckert, 2008b).

The most comprehensive UN convention on combating financing terrorism had been the convention that was adopted on November 9, 1999 and entered into force on April 10, 2002. The *United Nations Convention on the Prevention of Terrorist Financing of 1999 or New York Convention* was the most effective step taken before September 11, to combat on financing terrorism. According to convention, each state party had to; criminalize the financing of terrorism in their domestic law; detection, identification or freezing the funds allocated or used for terrorist purposed; whether the suspects involved in the terrorist financing crime are either prosecuted in accordance with their domestic law or extradited to the concerned country; in criminal investigations and prosecutions, cooperation with other countries; taking measures to ensure that financial institutions detect, and interfere and stop the flow of terrorist funds was foreseen (UN Resolution 54/109, 1999).

According to this Convention, which provides a categorical definition of financing terrorism, financing terrorism could be defined as;

Any person commits an offence within the meaning of this Convention if that person by any means, directly or indirectly, unlawfully and wilfully, provides or collects funds with the intention that they should be used or in the knowledge that they are to be used, in full or in part, in order to carry out:
a) An act which constitutes an offence within the scope of and as defined in one of the treaties listed in the annex; or
b) Any other act intended to cause death or serious bodily injury to a civilian, or to any other person not taking an active part in the hostilities in a situation of armed conflict, when the purpose of such act, by its nature or context, is to intimidate a population, or to compel a government or an international organization to do or to abstain from doing any act (UN Resolution 54/109, 1999).

On the other hand, in line with the New York Convention, the *UN Convention Against Transnational Organized Crime* was opened to signed in 2000 Palermo (Italy) and came to force in 2003. The purpose of this Convention is to promote cooperation to prevent and combat transnational organized crime more effectively. In this concept, the Convention suggested the state parties to criminalize illegal acts such as participation in organized crime groups, money laundering, corruption, and prevention of justice. However, in this Convention, the priority had given to the issues of corruption and money laundering in order to terrorism or financing terrorism (UNODC, 2004). In some cases, even if the offenses that mentioned in Convention are related to terrorism, in some cases only they are only related with organized crimes.

The September 11 attacks completely changed the world's view about terrorism. On September 12, the Security Council acted decisively and adopted *Resolution 1368*, establishing a legal basis for action against global terrorism. The Resolution was not directly related with financing terrorism but it suggested to all members of UN to being in cooperation with fighting against terrorism (UNSC, 2001a).

After the September 11 attacks, UNSC *Resolution 1373* was the most important decision taken by the UN in its history for fighting against terrorism on September 28. The Security Council took this decision unanimously and this Resolution focused every aspect of terrorism and put the financing terrorism on the beginning. According to Resolution 1373 all states shall;

a) Prevent and suppress the financing of terrorist acts;
b) Criminalize the willful provision or collection, by any means, directly or indirectly, of funds by their nationals or in their territories with the intention that the funds should be used, or in the knowledge that they are to be used, in order to carry out terrorist acts;
c) Freeze without delay funds and other financial assets or economic resources of persons who commit, or attempt to commit, terrorist acts or participate in or facilitate the commission of terrorist acts; of entities owned or controlled directly or indirectly by such persons; and of persons and entities acting on behalf of, or at the direction of such persons and entities, including funds derived or generated from property owned or controlled directly or indirectly by such persons and associated persons and entities;
d) Prohibit their nationals or any persons and entities within their territories from making any funds, financial assets or economic resources or financial or other related services available, directly or indirectly, for the benefit of persons who commit or attempt to commit or facilitate or participate in the commission of terrorist acts, of entities owned or controlled, directly or indirectly, by such persons and of persons and entities acting on behalf of or at the direction of such persons (UNSC, 2001b).

Also, on the article 6 of the Resolution established the *Counter Terrorism Committee* (hereinafter *CTC)* to bolster the ability of UN Member States to prevent terrorist acts both within their borders and across regions. It was established in the wake of the 11 September terrorist attacks in the US. The CTC is assisted by the Counter Terrorism Committee Executive Directorate (hereinafter CTED), which carries out the policy decisions of the Committee, conducts expert assessments of each Member State and facilitates counter-terrorism technical assistance to countries (UNSC Counter Terrorism Committee, 2017; UNSC, 2001b). The financing terrorism is one of the focusing areas of CTED, because according to CTED, the freezing of terrorist assets is a highly effective way for Member States to stem the flow of funds. Terrorism financing is a global phenomenon that not only threatens Member States' security but can also undermine economic development and financial market stability. It is therefore of paramount importance to stem the flow of funds to terrorists. Also, it is essential that Member States cooperate regionally and internationally, including through the exchange of operational information by relevant entities, especially national *FIUs* (UNSC Counter Terrorism Committee, 2017).

In fact, CTC is not the first committee established in this context. Even before the September 11 attacks, in 1999, with the UNSC *Resolution 1267* the council had demanded from member states to freeze funds and other financial resources directly or indirectly controlled by the Taliban. In addition, a pursuant committee was established to monitor sanctions against the Taliban, including the financial sector. Through this committee, a list of individuals and groups that financially sponsoring terrorism was issued, and all UN member states were obliged to confiscate the income of the persons or groups included in this list and prohibit the funds to be provided to these groups. Even the Taliban was the initial target of this committee, after September 11, the powers of Committee were increased, and the Security Council re-enforced sanctions and lists. In UNSC *Resolution 1363* the assets of Osama bin Laden and Al-Qaeda added to the list that would be frozen. In 2015 a new UNSC *Resolution 2253* was established and ISIL terrorist organization was added to list (UNSC, 2017).

The decisions that the UN had taken have brought about an effective mobilization of struggle against terrorism financing, not just in developed countries, but in almost all of the world. As it is known, security council decisions are binding. So, all member states were required to report to the CTC on the national measures taken to implement the resolution. Also, in that period many Asian states had made political and diplomatic initiatives to combat terrorism in all its aspects, including financing terrorism. Since the attacks of 11 September, there have been several international initiatives to counter-terrorist financing. International cooperation has given rise to a web of institutions and multilateral initiatives to suppress the financing of terrorism. But international cooperation and sanctions are a deep and comprehensive issue. For this reason, it is insufficient to examine only the activities of the UN to define the international measures against financing terrorism. Also, the activities of other international organizations need to be addressed.

2. Council of Europe

The oldest of the convention about combating terrorism by the Council of Europe, established in 1949, is the *European Convention on Suppression of Terrorism*, adopted in Strasbourg on 27 January 1977 (The Council of Europe, 1977). This Convention was being in force until amended by a Protocol that was adopted on 15 May 2003. In accordance with article 1/j of the Convention, which is added with Protocol, crimes within the scope of the "International Convention for the Suppression of Terrorism Financing adopted at New York on 9 December 1999" would not be considered as a political criminal (The Council of Europe, 2003).

On the other hand, *Convention on Laundering, Search, Seizure and Confiscation of the Proceeds from Crime or Strasbourg Convention* which was opened under the auspices of the Council of Europe on 8 November 1990 and which entered into force on 1 September 1993. One of the purposes of the Convention was to facilitate international co-operation for investigative assistance, search, seizure, and confiscation of the proceeds from all types of criminality, and in particular drug offenses, arms dealing, terrorist offenses, trafficking in children and young women, and other offenses which generate large profits. The Convention is intended to assist States in attaining a similar degree of efficiency even in the absence of full legislative harmony. Parties undertake in particular to criminalize the laundering of the proceeds of crime and to confiscate instrumentalities and proceeds (or property the value of which corresponds to such proceeds) (The Council of Europe, 1990).

On 2005, The Council of Europe decided to update its 1990 Convention to a new one, which was named also *Warsaw Convention*, to enhancing the efforts of Parties in preventing terrorism and its negative effects both by measures to be taken at national level and through international co-operation. In this convention definition of terrorist offenses was identified with the scope of the treaties listed in the Appendix. The appendix of Convention consists these international agreements:

1) Convention for the Suppression of Unlawful Seizure of Aircraft, signed at The Hague on 16 December 1970;
2) Convention for the Suppression of Unlawful Acts Against the Safety of Civil Aviation, concluded at Montreal on 23 September 1971;

3) Convention on the Prevention and Punishment of Crimes Against Internationally Protected Persons, Including Diplomatic Agents, adopted in New York on 14 December 1973;
4) International Convention Against the Taking of Hostages, adopted in New York on 17 December 1979
5) Convention on the Physical Protection of Nuclear Material, adopted in Vienna on 3 March 1980;
6) Protocol for the Suppression of Unlawful Acts of Violence at Airports Serving International Civil Aviation, done at Montreal on 24 February 1988;
7) Convention for the Suppression of Unlawful Acts Against the Safety of Maritime Navigation, done at Rome on 10 March 1988;
8) Protocol for the Suppression of Unlawful Acts Against the Safety of Fixed Platforms Located on the Continental Shelf, done at Rome on 10 March 1988;
9) International Convention for the Suppression of Terrorist Bombings, adopted in New York on 15 December 1997;
10) International Convention for the Suppression of the Financing of Terrorism, adopted in New York on 9 December 1999;
11) International Convention for the Suppression of Acts of Nuclear Terrorism, adopted in New York on 13 April 2005 (The Council of Europe, 2005a)

Because of these appendixes, accordingly to the provisions of the Convention shall apply to the acts of financing terrorism. In articles 5–8 it was emphasized that the acts as publicly terrorizing crimes, recruitment of terrorism, training for terrorism, and participating, organizing, and managing in these kind of activities would be accepted as terrorist offenses (The Council of Europe, 2005a).

Another important document within the Council of Europe is the *Council of Europe Convention on Laundering, Search, Seizure and Confiscation of the Proceeds from Crime and on the Financing of Terrorism*, according to UNSC Resolution 1373 and parallel to articles 2 and 4 of UN Convention on the Prevention of Terrorist Financing of 1999 or New York Convention. As a matter of fact, according to article 1/h of the Convention, the term "financing of terrorism" has been defined by article 2 of the New York Convention. The Convention generally introduced regulations in the field of combatting the crime. According to 2 Article of Convention, each party shall adopt such legislative and other measures as may be necessary to enable it to apply the provisions contained in Chapters III–V of this Convention to the financing of terrorism. In this context, each Party shall ensure that it is able to search, trace, identify, freeze, seize, and confiscate property, of a licit or illicit origin, used or allocated to be used by any means, in whole or in part, for the financing of terrorism, or the proceeds of this offense, and to provide co-operation to this end to the widest possible extent. In Chapter IV, the Convention had emphasized the international cooperation in the scope of investigative assistance, provisional measures, confiscation, situations related with refusal, and postponement of co-operation and notification and protection of third parties' rights. The important thing in this convention was the separation of financing terrorism from other offenses. In the article 28 of the Convention was specified the conditions that could include, the refusal of cooperation in case of the offense to which the request relates is a fiscal offence, with the exception of the financing of terrorism (The Council of Europe, 2005b).

On 2015 the Council of Europe established an *Additional Protocol to the Council of Europe Convention on the Prevention of Terrorism* for the purpose of supplementing the provisions of the Council of Europe Convention on the Prevention of Terrorism, opened for signature in Warsaw on 16 May 2005 as regards the criminalization of the acts described in Articles 2 to 6 of this Protocol. Also, the other purpose was enhancing the efforts of Parties in preventing terrorism and its negative effects on the full enjoyment of human rights, in particular the right to life, both by measures to be taken at national level and through international co-operation, with due regard to the existing applicable multilateral or bilateral treaties or agreements between the Parties. In this context, the new Protocol especially focused the areas of participating in an association or group for the purpose of terrorism, receiving training for terrorism, travelling abroad for the purpose of terrorism, funding travelling abroad for the purpose of terrorism, and organizing or otherwise facilitating travelling abroad for the purpose of terrorism (The Council of Europe, 2015).

The Council of Europe, which was founded in 1949, was institution that to had taken the earliest measures against terrorism in continental Europe. However, in the following period, the Council of Europe had been left behind to other international organizations such as the UN and the EU, mostly producing conventions or agreements that govern the policies in the international community.

3. European Union

Fighting against both terrorism and its financial aspects is not a new issue in the EU, one of the most influential institutions in the international community. Even if it is an economic-based organization, the community has never ignored the "security" issues, which is always affect economic co-operation. The first initiative about anti-money laundering (AML) in EU, *Prevention of The Use of the Financial System for the Purpose of Money Laundering* was introduced in 1991 and contained several important features that are now regarded as the benchmark in the preventative measures used to combat money laundering. In particular, the relevant features of the Money Laundering Directive were the need to ensure client identification, the examination and reporting of suspicious transactions, indemnities to be given for good faith reporting of suspicious transactions, identification records to be kept for five years after the client relationship has ended, cooperation with the authorities and adequate internal procedures and training programmes to be adopted. It is important to note that this Directive concentrated on the "combating the laundering of drug proceeds though the financial sector", and not the financing of terrorism (91/308/EEC, 1991).

On 1999, with the decision of European Commission (hereinafter EC), EU established the *European Anti-Fraud Office (OLAF)* for investigates fraud against the EU budget, corruption, and serious misconduct within the European institutions, and develops anti-fraud policy for the EC. In the articles 3rd and 4th of the decision, the reasons of why the union need OLAF was explained as; the need to increase the effectiveness of the fight against fraud and other illegal activities detrimental to the financial interests of the Communities requires the establishment of a OLAF, which must exercise its investigation powers in full independence (1999/352/EC, 1999). Just before the September 11 attacks, in 2000 the European Council introduced the decision about *Concerning Arrangements for Cooperation Between FIUs of the Member States in Respect of Exchanging Information* which was primarily focused on cooperation's of FIUs of all member states (2000/642/JHA, 2000). In the same year Council take a framework decision on *Money Laundering, the Identification, Tracing, Freezing, Seizing and Confiscation of Instrumentalities and The Proceeds of Crime* with the reservations in respect of the 1990 Convention of the Council of Europe as we explained above. According to Framework decision, in order to enhance action against organized crime, Member States shall take the necessary steps not to make or uphold reservations in respect of the following articles of the 1990 Convention. According to Framework,

> Each Member State shall take the necessary steps to ensure that its legislation and procedures on the confiscation of the proceeds of crime also allow, at least in cases where these proceeds cannot be seized, for the confiscation of property the value of which corresponds to such proceeds, both in purely domestic proceedings and in proceedings instituted at the request of another Member State, including requests for the enforcement of foreign confiscation orders. However, Member States may exclude the confiscation of property the value of which corresponds to the proceeds of crime in cases in which that value would be less than EUR 4000. The words 'property', 'proceeds' and 'confiscation' shall have the same meaning as in Article 1 of the 1990 Convention (2001/500/JHA, 2001).

As it was seen that, it is possible to say that, before the September 11 attacks, the vast majority of decisions taken within the EU were related to financial crimes in general, aside from financing terrorism. However, after the September 11 attacks, EU has also changed its outlook to the international terrorism, as in the whole world. In this context, the increasing importance of fighting against financing terrorism has emerged in that period.

After September 11, it became clear that the scope of the 1991 Directive was too narrow and ineffective. Therefore, the EU introduced a broader Second Money Laundering Directive, named as *Directive 2001/97/EC of the European Parliament and of The Council of 4 December 2001 Amending Council Directive 91/308/EEC on Prevention of the Use of the Financial System for The Purpose of Money Laundering*, which increased the list of predicate offences for which the suspicious transaction reports (hereinafter STRs) were compulsory, from just drug trafficking offences to all serious criminal offences and extended the scope of the Directive to a number of professions and non-financial activities. Also, the Directive envisages the fulfilment of obligations, to prevent money laundering by those who were engaged in credit institutions, financial institutions, auditors, accountants, financial advisers, notaries, and independent law professions, real estate agents, casinos and the sale of precious stones, mines, artwork, and auctions that carry over 15,000 euros in cash (2001/97/EC, 2001).

In fact, after the September 11 attacks, the EU had made many attempts to combat terrorism. Some of these were the general measures aimed at the whole of the aspects of terrorism, while others included and focused on the measures to prevent the financing terrorism. For example, the EU has implemented a series of countering financing terrorism (hereinafter CFT) measures following the terrorist attacks in September 2001. On 27 December 2001, the European Council published *its Council Common Position on Combatting Terrorism*, which focused the big picture of terrorist offenses but on the other hand the Common Position starts with the issues about CFT measures. According to Common position member states were required to adopt broad principles of liability to be applied to natural or legal persons who assist in the funding of terrorism, and the importance of this Common Position cannot be underestimated because its "purpose was to implement UN Security Council Resolution 1373" as we explained above. In addition, the member states were invited to become parties to the international agreements attached to the document as soon as possible (2001/930/CFSP, 2001). On the same date EU also introduced some other documents as: *Council Common Position on the Application of Specific Measure to Combat Terrorism* for the purpose of the freezing of the funds and other financial assets or economic resources of persons, groups, and entities listed in the Annex of document, reviewed them at regular intervals and at least once every six months to ensure that there are grounds for keeping them on the list, and through police and judicial cooperation in criminal matters within the framework of Title VI of the Treaty on EU, afford each other the widest possible assistance in preventing and combating terrorist acts (2001/931/CFSP, 2001). In the context of this Common Position, on the same date the EU published a Council Regulation *Specific Restrictive Measures Directed Against Certain Persons and Entities with a View to Combating Terrorism* was accepted in order to comply with the UN Security Council Resolution 1373. According to Regulation the Council, acting by unanimity, shall establish, review, and amend the list of persons, groups and entities to which this Regulation applies, in accordance with the provisions laid down in Article 1 of Common Position 2001/931/CFSP and the Commission shall be empowered, on the basis of information supplied by Member States, to amend the Annex (EC No 2580/2001, 2001).

This Regulation and Common positions was followed a year later by the adoption of a new *Council Regulation (EC) No 881/2002 Of 27 May 2002 Imposing Certain Specific Restrictive Measures Directed Against Certain Persons and Entities Associated with Usama bin Laden, The Al-Qaida Network and The Taliban, And Repealing Council Regulation (EC) No 467/2001 Prohibiting the Export of Certain Goods and Services to Afghanistan, Strengthening the Flight Ban and Extending the Freeze of Funds and Other Financial Resources in Respect of the Taliban of Afghanistan* which contains a "black list" of names, which duplicates those designated by the UN Sanctions Committee. That was a long "black list" but there is some famous entities or interesting countries that challenge the EU as; most of the Al Barakaat Bank, Finance Group, Financial Holdings, Group Companies in Dubai, Somalia, USA, UAE; Bank Al Taqwa in Bahamas; Barakaat Trading, International Foundation, North America, Telecommunication, Banks and Remittances, Computer consulting in Dubai, USA, UAE, Somalia; Somali International Relief Organization in USA; Youssef M. Nada & Co. Gesellschaft in Austria or Youssef M. Nada, and Via Riasc in Switzerland (EC No 881/2002, 2002).

In 2004, the EC determined that it was necessary to introduce a Third Money Laundering Directive, to replace the First Directive and amend the Second Directive. With the *Directive 2005/60/EC of the European Parliament and of the Council of 26 October 2005 on the Prevention of the Use of the Financial System for the Purpose of Money Laundering and Terrorist Financing*, stated that Member States should make the necessary arrangements to prevent money laundering and financing terrorism. Directive defined, the offenses set forth in the Council

Framework Decision 2002/475/JHA, the 1988 UN Vienna Convention on Drug Abuse, Fraud and corruption offenses, Freedoms are punishable by more than one year, or the lower limit of punishment is six months or more as a predicate offences and (1) credit institutions; (2) financial institutions; (3) the following legal or natural persons acting in the exercise of their professional activities: (a) auditors, external accountants, and tax advisors; (b) notaries and other independent legal professionals, when they participate, whether by acting on behalf of and for their client in any financial or real estate transaction, or by assisting in the planning or execution of transactions for their client concerning the: (i) buying and selling of real property or business entities; (ii) managing of client money, securities or other assets; (iii) opening or management of bank, savings or securities accounts; (iv) organization of contributions necessary for the creation, operation or management of companies; (v) creation, operation, or management of trusts, companies or similar structures; (c) trust or company service providers not already covered under points (a) or (b); (d) real estate agents; (e) other natural or legal persons trading in goods, only to the extent that payments are made in cash in an amount of EUR 15,000 or more, whether the transaction is executed in a single operation or in several operations which appear to be linked; (f) casinos were obliged to be liable. The Third Directive was introduced for a wide range of reasons including the narrow scope of the Second Directive and had effect across all members of the EU and the European Economic Area. Furthermore, and importantly the Third Money Laundering Directive directly refers to the prohibition of money laundering and terrorist financing. This is an important step in the evolution of the EU's CFT strategy. Also, the Directive defines the cases and measures of the institutions and persons had to apply the CDD measures as when establishing a business relationship; when carrying out occasional transactions amounting to EUR 15,000 or more; when there is a suspicion of money laundering or terrorist financing, regardless of any derogation, exemption or threshold and when there are doubts about the veracity or adequacy of previously obtained customer identification data. On the other hand, the Directive emphasized again establishing a FIU in order to effectively to combat money laundering and terrorist financing. Last with this Directive, the Commission would be assisted by a "Committee on the Prevention of Money Laundering and Terrorist Financing" (2005/60/EC, 2005).

The recent terrorist attacks highlighted the need for the EU to take further measures and step up its fight against money laundering and terrorism financing. The adoption of the Fourth Anti-Money Laundering Directive; the *Directive (EU) 2015/849 of the European Parliament and of the Council of 20 May 2015 on the*

Prevention of the Use of the Financial System for the Purposes of Money Laundering or Terrorist Financing, Amending Regulation (EU) No 648/2012 of the European Parliament and of the Council, and Repealing Directive 2005/60/EC of The European Parliament and of the Council and Commission Directive 2006/70/EC aimed to prevent the use of the Union's financial system for the purposes of money laundering and terrorist financing. It was a major step forward in improving the effectiveness of the EU's efforts to combat the laundering of money from criminal activities and to counter the financing of terrorist activities and set high standards to ensure that credit and financial institutions are equipped to detect and acted against such risks. This Directive, which requires Member States to fulfil necessary laws, regulations, and administrative provisions till 26 June 2017 mainly focused on applying enhanced checks ("due diligence measures/counter-measures") toward high-risk third countries; bring virtual currency exchange platforms under the scope of the Directive; strengthen transparency measures applicable to prepaid instruments, such as prepaid cards, by lowering thresholds for identification from €250 to €150 and widening customer verification requirements; enhance the powers of FIU's and facilitate their cooperation by further aligning the rules for such Units with the latest international standards and give FIU's swift access to information on the holders of bank-and payment accounts, through centralized registers or electronic data retrieval systems (EU 2015/849, 2015).

4. Financial Action Task Force (FATF) and FATF Style Regional Bodies (FSRBs)

The FATF is an inter-governmental body established by the G-7 Summit that was held in Paris in 1989 by the Ministers of its Member jurisdictions in response to mounting concern over money laundering. Recognizing the threat posed to the banking system and to financial institutions, the G-7 Heads of State or Government and President of the EC convened the Task Force from the G-7 member States, the EC and 8 other countries. According to the article 53 of G-7 Paris Summit;

> Convene a financial action task force from Summit participants and other countries interested in these problems. Its mandate is to assess the results of cooperation already undertaken in order to prevent the utilization of the banking system and financial institutions for the purpose of money laundering, and to consider additional preventive efforts in this field, including the adaptation of the legal and regulatory systems so as to enhance multilateral judicial assistance. The first meeting of this task force will be called by France and its report will be completed by April 1990 (G-7 Summit, 1989).

While operating under the framework of the Organization for Economic Co-operation and Development (hereinafter OECD), it is not an organ of the OECD but works independently. The secretariat of FATF is in Paris. When FATF was established the main aims of the organization were: giving the message to the whole world to take measures against money laundering, based on the enlargement of FATF membership, supporting worldwide initiatives against money laundering, and monitoring money laundering techniques and trends, and to develop measures against it. However just after September 11 attacks, the issues related with CFT was included between the objectives of FATF. Today the objectives of the FATF can be described as setting the standards and promote effective implementation of legal, regulatory, and operational measures for combating money laundering, terrorist financing, and other related threats to the integrity of the international financial system.

The FATF currently comprises of 35 member jurisdictions and 2 regional organizations, representing most major financial centers in all parts of the globe. The members are: Argentina, Australia, Austria, Belgium, Brazil, Canada, China, Denmark, EC, Finland, France, Germany, Greece, Gulf Co-operation Council, Hong Kong, China, Iceland, India, Ireland, Italy, Japan, Republic of Korea, Luxembourg, Malaysia, Mexico, Netherlands, Kingdom of, New Zealand, Norway, Portugal, Russian Federation, Singapore, South Africa, Spain, Sweden, Switzerland, Turkey, the UK, and the US. Israel and Saudi Arabia are the FATF Observers countries and Asia/Pacific Group (APG) on Money Laundering, Caribbean Financial Action Task Force (CFATF), MONEYVAL, Eurasian Group (EAG), Eastern and Southern Africa Anti-Money Laundering Group (ESAAMLG), Financial Action Task Force of Latin America (GAFILAT) (formerly known as Financial Action Task Force on Money Laundering in South America (GAFISUD)), Intergovernmental Action Group against Money Laundering in West Africa (GIABA), Middle East and North Africa Financial Action Task Force (MENAFATF), and Task Force on Money Laundering in Central Africa (GABAC) are also Associate Members or FATF Style Regional Bodies (hereinafter FSRBs) of FATF. Beside Associate Members there are many international organizations who have observer status with the FATF those which have, among other functions, a specific AML mission or function.

The FATF is therefore a "policy-making body" which works to generate the necessary political will to bring about national legislative and regulatory reforms in these areas. The FATF has developed a series of Recommendations that are recognized as the international standard for combating of money laundering and the financing of terrorism and proliferation of WMD. It is an inter-governmental body whose function is to development and promotes AML. It is important to note, that the FATF is not a law-making body, but "it does make recommendations that have a global reach".

They form the basis for a coordinated response to these threats to the integrity of the financial system and help ensure a level playing field. First issued in 1990 mainly focused on general framework of the recommendations, improvement of national legal systems to combat money laundering, enhancement of the role of the financial system, strengthening of international cooperation (FATF, 1990), and the FATF Recommendations were revised in 1996, 2001, 2003, and most recently in 2012 to ensure that they remain up to date and relevant, and they are intended to be of universal application. The latest recommendation consisted seven sections and subsections about; AML/CTF policies and coordination, AML/CTF policies and coordination, terrorist financing and financing of proliferation, preventive measures, transparency and beneficial ownership of legal persons and arrangements, powers and responsibilities of competent authorities, and other institutional measures and international cooperation (FATF, 2012). These Recommendations have been widely accepted as the international AML and counter-terrorist financing standard and approved by more than 170 countries. The FATF also carries out cross-country reviews of measures taken to implement particular Recommendations (Ryder, 2015).

As mentioned above financing terrorism had been discussed in FATF for a prior to September 11, but the attacks prompted a formal expansion of the FATF's mandate in October 2001, resulting in the elaboration of *Special Recommendations on Terrorist Financing* (FATF, 2001). The organization's approach to countering the financing of global terrorism changed dramatically after 11 September 2001. FATF Special Recommendations on Terrorist Financing recognizing the vital importance of acting to combat the financing of terrorism. The nine special recommendations are;

I.   Ratification and implementation of UN instruments.
II.   Criminalizing the financing of terrorism and associated money laundering.
III.   Freezing and confiscating terrorist assets.
IV.   Reporting suspicious transactions related to terrorism.
V.   International Co-operation.
VI.   Alternative Remittance.
VII.   Wire transfers.
VIII.   Non-profit organizations.
IX.   Cash Couriers Countries.

According to this Special Recommendations, each country should take immediate steps to ratify and to implement fully the 1999 UN International Convention for the Suppression of the Financing of Terrorism. Countries should also immediately implement the UN resolutions relating to the prevention and suppression of the financing of terrorist acts, particularly UN Security Council Resolution 1373. Each country should criminalize the financing of terrorism, terrorist acts and terrorist organizations and should ensure that such offences are designated as money laundering predicate offences. Each country should implement measures to freeze without delay funds or other assets of terrorists, those who finance terrorism and terrorist organizations. If financial institutions, or other businesses or entities subject to AML obligations, suspect or have reasonable grounds to suspect that funds are linked or related to, or are to be used for terrorism, terrorist acts or by terrorist organizations, they should be required to report promptly their suspicions to the competent authorities. Each country should afford another country, on the basis of a treaty, arrangement or other mechanism for mutual legal assistance or information exchange, the greatest possible measure of assistance in connection with criminal, civil enforcement, and administrative investigations, inquiries and proceedings relating to the financing of terrorism, and terrorist acts and terrorist organizations. Each country should take measures to ensure that persons or legal entities, including agents, that provide a service for the transmission of money or value, including transmission through an informal money or value transfer system or network, should be licensed or registered, and subject to all the FATF Recommendations that apply to banks and non-bank financial institutions. Countries should take measures to require financial institutions, including money remitters, to include accurate and meaningful originator information (name, address and account number) on funds transfers and related messages that are sent, and the information should remain with the transfer or related message through the payment chain. Countries should review the adequacy of laws and regulations that relate to entities that can be abused for the financing of terrorism. Non-profit organizations are particularly vulnerable, and countries should ensure that they cannot be misused. Countries should have measures in place to detect the physical cross-border transportation of currency and bearer negotiable instruments, including a declaration system or other disclosure obligation (FATF, 2001).

On the other hand, in FATF prepared Non-Cooperative Countries and Territories (NCCT) initiative (2000–2001) for the aim of the NCCT Initiative was to reduce the vulnerability of the financial system to money laundering by ensuring that all financial centers adopt and implement measures for the prevention, detection, and punishment of money laundering according to internationally recognized standards.

The FATF monitors the progress of its members in implementing necessary measures, reviews money laundering, terrorist financing techniques, and counter-measures, and promotes the adoption and implementation of appropriate measures globally. In collaboration with other international stakeholders, the FATF works to identify national-level vulnerabilities with the aim of protecting the international financial system from misuse. Since its inception, the FATF has operated under a fixed life-span, requiring a specific decision by its Ministers to continue. The current mandate of the FATF (2012–2020) was adopted at a Ministerial meeting in April 2012.

On the other hand, FSRBs is the general name given to the bodies that countries in various geographical parts of the world come together to form in order to work within a program so as to fight with the money laundering (and financing of terrorism). FATF is a standard-setting pioneer body in the fight against money laundering and financing of terrorism whose members range from New Zealand to Iceland, Republic of South Africa to Canada, which are all major developed countries of the world. FSRBs are, on the other hand, bodies that ensure that countries close to each other in geographical position implement their struggle together within a group procedure. FSRBs include FATF member states; however, a majority of members of these bodies are not FATF members. FATF Style Regional Bodies are making reference to the FATF standards and other international norms in their fight against money laundering and financing of terrorism and evaluate the activities of its members with "mutual valuation process" which is similar to FATF practice.

Below are FATF Style Bodies:

1. APG on Money Laundering
2. CFATF
3. ESAAMLG
4. GAFISUD
5. MENAFATF
6. MONEYVAL
7. GIABA
8. Eurasian Group
9. Off-Shore Group Banking Supervisory (OGBS)

Asia Pacific Group on Money Laundering
APG was founded according to the decision taken at the fourth Asia Pacific Money Laundering Symposium which was held in February 1997 in Bangkok

with the purpose of fighting with money laundering on a regional scale. The group refers to the standards in the Forty Recommendations of FATF; later it included financing of terrorism into its area of activity. As the case in FATF, it measures the activities of its members through mutual evaluation process.

The secretariat of the group is in Sydney, and its members are as follows: Afghanistan, Australia, Bangladesh, Brunei Sultanate, Cambodia, Canada, Taiwan, Cook Islands, Fiji, Hong Kong-China, India, Indonesia, Japan, Laos, Macao-China, Malaysia, Marshall Islands, Mongolia, Myanmar, Nauru, Nepal, New Zealand, Niue, Pakistan, Republic of Korea, Palau, Philippines, Samoa, Singapore, Sri Lanka, Solomon Islands, Thailand, Tonga, USA, Vanuatu, and Vietnam. APG became a privileged member of FATF in 2006 (APG, 2017).

Caribbean Financial Action Task Force
CFATF is a FATF Style body consisting of the thirty countries in Caribbean basin which was established with the purpose of fighting with money laundering. CFATF was founded as a result of the decisions taken at May 1990 Aruba and November 1992 Jamaica meetings and it accepted a memorandum of understanding stating that it adopted UN Vienna Convention and FATF Forty Recommendations. CFATF later added to its missions fighting with financing of terrorism.

The secretariat of the group is in Trinidad & Tobago, and its members are as follows: Antigua & Barbuda, Anguilla, Aruba, Bahamas, Barbados, Belize, Bermuda, British Virgin islands', Cayman Islands, Costa Rica, Dominic, Dominic Republic, El Salvador, Grenada, Guatemala, Guyana, Haiti, Honduras, Jamaica, Montserrat, Netherlands Antilles, Nicaragua, Panama, St. Kitts-Nevis, St. Lucia, St. Vincent & Grenadines, Surinam, Trinidad & Tobago, and Turks & Caicos Islands and Venezuela (CFATF, 2017).

Eastern and Southern Africa Anti-Money Laundering Group (ESAAMLG)
ESAAMLG was established at the meeting held in Arusha (Tanzania) on 26–27 August 1999 with the purpose of fighting with money laundering. Later it included financing of terrorism into its area of activity.

The secretariat of the group is in Darussalam (Tanzania), and its members are as follows: Botswana, Kenya, Malawi, Mauritius, Mozambique, Namibia, Seychelles, South African Republic, Swaziland, Tanzania, Uganda, Lesotho, Zambia, and Zimbabwe (ESAAMLG, 2017).

FATF on Money Laundering in South America (GAFISUD)
FATF on Money Laundering in South America was founded on 8 December 2000 in Cartagena (Colombia) with a memorandum of understanding prepared by the representatives of nine South American countries with the purpose of

fighting with money laundering. Later GAFISUD included financing of terrorism into its area of activity.

The secretariat of GAFISUD is in Buenos Aires, and its members are as follows: Argentina, Bolivia, Brazil, Chile, Colombia, Ecuador, Mexico, Paraguay, Peru, Uruguay, Organization of American States (OAS), and Inter-American Drug Abuse Control Commission (CI-CAD) is consultant member of the body. GAFISUD became a privileged member of FATF in 2006 (GAFILAT, 2017).

MONEYVAL
MONEYVAL was founded with the transformation into MONEYVAL in 2002 by European Council Committee of Ministers of PC-R-EV (Select Committee of Experts on the Evaluation of Anti Money laundering Measures) established in September 1997 by FATF nom-members of Council member countries with the purpose of developing capacity of fighting with money laundering. In the process of evaluating its member countries, MONEYVAL makes references to 1988 dated Vienna Convention, FATF recommendation, European Council Conventions and EU Directives. It extended its area of activity to include fighting with financing of terrorism after 11 September 2001. The secretariat of MONEYVAL is in Strasbourg, and its members are as follows: Albania, Andorra, Armenia, Azerbaijan, Bosnia-Herzegovina, Bulgaria, France, the Netherlands, Croatia, Cyprus (Greek Administration), Czech Republic, Estonia, Georgia, Hungary, Latvia, Liechtenstein, Lithuania, Moldova, Malta, Monaco, Poland, Romania, Russian Federation, San Marino, Serbia, Montenegro, Slovakia, Slovenia, Macedonia, and Ukraine. FATF is being represented in MONEYVAL by France and the Netherlands. MONEYVAL was accepted as a privileged member to FATF in 2006 (MONEYVAL, 2017).

Eurasian Group (EAG)
EAG was founded based on the decision given at Moscow Conference which was held on 6 October 2004. EAG was accepted as an observer state to FATF in 2004 General Board meeting. Belarus, China, Kazakhstan, Kyrgyzstan, Russian federation, Tajikistan, and Uzbekistan are members of EAG whose secretariat is in Moscow. Turkey became an observer state to EAG in December 2005 (EAG, 2017).

Middle East and North Africa Financial Action Force (MENAFATF)
Foundation of MENAFATF was decided at a meeting of ministers of 14 countries (Jordan, UAE, Bahrain, Tunisia, Algeria, Saudi Arabia, Syria, Oman, Qatar, Kuwait, Lebanon, Egypt, Morocco, and Yemen) which was held in Manama (Bahrain) on 30 November 2004. The secretariat of MENAFATF is in Bahrain and its members are as follows: Jordan, UAE, Bahrain, Tunisia, Algeria, Saudi

Arabia, Syria, Oman, Qatar, Kuwait, Lebanon, Egypt, Morocco, Yemen, Mauritania, and Iraq. MENAFATF became a privileged member of FATF in 2007 (MENAFATF, 2017).

Intergovernmental Group on Anti Money Laundering in Africa (GIABA)
GIABA was founded in November 2000 upon decision taken in December 1999 in Lomé (Togo) at the summit held by the heads of government and states of Economic Community of West African States (ECOWAS) member states. The secretariat of Dakar (Senegal) and its members are as follows: Benin, Burkina Faso, Cape Verde, Ivory Coast, Gambia, Ghana, Guinea-Bissau, Guinea -Conakry, Liberia, Mali, Niger, Nigeria, Senegal, Sierra Leone, and Togo.

The group adopted the FATF Forty Recommendations at its first meeting and accepted a directive which envisages the regulations on fighting with money laundering and financing of terrorism in its Council of Minister meetings on 19 September 2002 (GIABA, 2017).

Off-Shore Group Banking Supervisory (OGBS)
OGBS was established under the leadership of Basel Committee in October 1980. It is an observer member of FATF and it was given the FATF style body by FATF. The group serves its functions according to the following purposes:

- Discussing and identifying mutual areas of interests of its members,
- Sharing knowledge and experiences,
- Ensuring that international standards are implemented in fighting with money laundering and financing of terrorism as well as off-shore banking areas and participating in international bodies established for this purpose,
- Encouraging it members to implement internationally accepted supervision and monitoring standards and adopting and developing constructive and positive recommendations made by other supervisory and monitoring authorities in the areas of supervision and monitoring of international banking. The members of the group are as follows: Aruba, Bahamas, Bahrain, Barbados, Bermuda, Cayman Islands, Cyprus (Greek Administration), Gibraltar, Guernsey, Hong Kong, Isle of Man, Jersey, Labuan, Macau-China, Mauritius, Netherlands Antilles, Panama, Singapore, and Vanuatu. The chair of the group settles in Jersey.

Chapter III. The Role FININT Can Play

The establishment of an effective system for the prevention of money laundering and terrorist financing is based on:

- Adoption of a legislative framework for the prevention of money laundering and terrorist financing (*incrimination, strategy, legal remedies, by-laws, etc.*)
- The role of the obligated entities (financial and non-financial institutions) that have the authority to undertake measures and actions for the prevention of money laundering and terrorist financing.
- Establishing a FIU and defining its role (*administrative, law enforcement, judicial or hybrid type*).
- Identifying and prosecuting perpetrators of criminal offences involving money laundering and terrorist financing (*cooperation and exchange of information between institutions at national and international level*).

1. Legislative Framework

As mentioned in the preceding chapters, the fight against terrorist financing is quite complex and requires a multidimensional approach. This fight is not only focused on terrorist financing, but also on money laundering and other crimes that generate illegal income which can be used to finance terrorism. Since it is about two distinct processes that at a given moment can be kinetically related, i.e., money laundering can be used in the process of terrorist financing, the measures and actions that are being undertaken should be directed toward both processes. Therefore, the fulfillment of the undertaken obligations for the prevention of money laundering and terrorist financing should be one of the national priorities of every country. To that end, countries should sign and ratify international documents as a basis for adopting numerous legal remedies for incriminating money laundering and terrorist financing, as well as confiscating proceeds that have been acquired by criminal offences. In addition, it is necessary to draw up several strategic documents in the field of judiciary, internal affairs and security-intelligence systems, money laundering and terrorist financing, terrorism and extremism, etc. In order to prevent money laundering and terrorist financing, it is necessary to adopt the following legal instruments:

- **Law on the prevention of money laundering and terrorist financing**
- **National risk assessment of money laundering and terrorist financing**

- **National Strategy for the prevention of money laundering and terrorist financing**
- **An action plan** for the implementation of the strategy
- **By-laws**
- **Law on international restrictive measures (sanctions)** that will implement sanctions imposed by international organizations at the request of third countries.

The process of combating terrorist financing requires not just one person or institution but a system which defines the risks, the competent institutions, and the implementation of measures and actions for the prevention, detection, and prosecution of persons who have committed, are in progress of committing or plan to commit such an act.

In the fight against terrorist financing, three categories of entities have been engaged:

- <u>Obligated entities</u> in accordance with the legislation
- <u>FIU</u> and other competent state agencies
- <u>Other natural and legal persons</u> whose obligations are prescribed by the legislation regulating the implementation of international restrictive measures (sanctions) imposed by international organizations, third countries, or internal sanctions imposed by competent state agencies.

2. The Role of Obligated Entities (Financial and Non-Financial Institutions)

In order to attract more customers and gain larger profits, financial and non-financial institutions are in constant competition to modernize, innovate and market new products that will satisfy the everyday needs of their customers. In the previous chapters, through practical examples, we confirmed that these institutions were used and abused by criminals for the purpose of money laundering or terrorist financing in all their phases, placement, layering, and integration.

In order to minimize or eliminate the risk of involvement or abuse of these institutions in both processes, the international community has established the FATF on money laundering. Monitoring and revealing the types of money laundering and terrorist financing, this body has set a series of standards, i.e., measures and actions that should be undertaken by countries, that is, from all concerned and involved institutions and natural persons, including financial and non-financial institutions. Therefore, all legal and natural persons that should employ the measures and actions for preventing money laundering and terrorist financing are included in the category of obligated entities. Any deviation from or non-application of the measures and actions exposes the entity to the risk of involvement in money laundering or terrorist financing. According to the Basel Committee on Banking Supervision, the obligated entity can face four types of risks that will adversely affect its future performance. These are: *reputational, operational, legal and concentration risks* (Basel Committee for Banking Supervision, 2000). Because banking institutions are most involved and abused in money laundering and terrorist financing processes, they are also most afraid of these risks.

- Reputational risk – The bank's work is of a long-term character, and its survival on the market depends on the building of trust between the bank and the client which is a key driver for creating a good image and reputation of the bank. In order to protect itself from adverse consequences that will tarnish its image and reputation, the bank must introduce norms and standards for establishing a business relationship with its clients. From that aspect, banks and other financial institutions must introduce strict rules and programs through which they will inform themselves about their client before establishing a business relationship, as well as monitor his activities within that business relationship in order to determine suspicious or unusual transactions and activities that deviate from everyday work, and may be related to money laundering and terrorist financing. If these measures are not implemented, the credit rating of the bank may decrease and clients may withdraw their funds, thereby losing some of them, which will reflect on the economic performance of the bank with the prospect of its closing and liquidation.
- Operational risk – The conduct of preventive policy is a condition for reducing all types of risks including operational risk. This means that any untimely implementation of appropriate measures and actions for preventing a negative occurrence, or risk, will lead to an increase in the cost of its fixing. The operational risk is directly affected by the development of the technical and administrative capacities of the bank. Namely, inadequate equipment, substandard and untrained personnel subject to corrupt deals, and lack of internal control will take the bank into operational risk, thereby committing crimes by its involvement in the processes of money laundering and terrorist financing.
- Legal risk – By not taking measures and actions to prevent money laundering and terrorist financing, the bank may be involved in the same processes that represent criminal offences. Therefore, the bank may be prosecuted in court for not taking appropriate measures and actions. This, in turn, can cause a domino effect through legal obstacles to the fulfillment of the obligations that

the bank has toward its customers or business partners, which further increases the risk.

- Concentration risk – The concentration risk results from the occurrence of previous risks. This means that all these risks are intertwined and mutually dependent. Taking into account the previous risks, the bank can find itself in a situation where customers will withdraw their deposits and money from their accounts, decreasing the financial stability and power of the bank; thus, reducing the possibility of their placement as loans, investments, etc.

In general, the measures and actions that should be undertaken by entities are reduced to four categories:

- *Customer analysis*
- *Monitoring certain transactions*
- *Gathering, storing, and submitting data for transactions and clients for which there are grounds for suspicion of money laundering and terrorist financing*
- *Introduction and implementation of programs.*

2.1 Customer Analysis

Taking into consideration the phases of money laundering and terrorist financing, as well as the possibility of involvement and abuse of the bank and other financial institutions in these processes, and the prevention should start when the business relation between the customer and the bank is established. When establishing a business relation with the client, the bank should use the appropriate procedures for customer identification (Know Your Customer Procedure) regardless of whether it is a natural or legal person. The implementation of these procedures should enable banks to be sure they know their customers and that the establishment of a business relation does not carry risks for the bank. On the other hand, we already explained the risks to the banks in case of not taking appropriate measures and actions.

Banks and other obligated entities have a duty to conduct customer analysis in the following cases:

- *In the process of establishing a business relation*
- *When performing one or related transactions in the amount of 15,000 EUR*
- *When there are grounds for suspicion of money laundering and terrorist financing*
- *When there is doubt about the truthfulness and adequacy of the previously obtained customer identity data.*

When performing the customer analysis and customer acceptance procedure, banks, and other entities are required to determine the identity of the customer, the proxy and the end user, and to confirm their identity, provide data about the intention of the business relation, and to continuously monitor the business relation and its transactions in order to ensure that they are consistent with the risk profile and the customer's line of work. In certain cases, the bank is required to determine the true origin of the funds, i.e., the sources of funding.

Also, when conducting customer analysis and acceptance procedures, the bank is required to determine whether the customer has been or is involved in criminal activities, whether he/she is a Politically Exposed Person (hereinafter PEP), the region or country of origin, and to search the lists of terrorists and terrorist organizations published by international organizations. In the first chapter we explained the significance of knowing the areas where terrorist organizations operate. In this context, of particular importance to the bank is determining the customer's place, region, or country of origin in order to obtain more information about whether he/she is a member of a terrorist organization, thereby verifying or rejecting the establishment of a business relation.

2.1.1 Customer Profiling

Profiling of high-risk customers is of great importance for the financial institution, in this particular case, the bank, in order to determine the potential risk of establishing a business relation with them. In a situation of fierce competition for attracting customers, upon which the profit of the bank also depends, the question that arises is whether the bank has an interest in establishing business relations with customers who represent potential risks. The answer depends on the internal business policy of the bank, how much it is willing to bear the burden called "risky client", while consciously or unconsciously damaging its reputational risk, as well as the security risk in the country itself. As an illustration, if the bank establishes a business relation with a customer on a sanctions list, not only the bank but also the country will bear the consequences, internationally, because it has not taken appropriate measures to prevent this and to ensure its own safety.

Managing risky clients is extremely important for the bank. If the bank establishes a business relation with a customer categorized as risky, he/she should be constantly monitored by an authorized person, or his/her deputy, or, if legally established, by the special department for preventing money laundering and terrorist financing of the bank. This department is obligated to monitor the customer's business activities and if it determines transactions or activities that deviate from the day-to-day operations, or there are indicators for suspicious transactions, it is required to prepare a report on suspicious transactions and submit it to the FIU.

From the aspect of detecting and preventing terrorist financing, the bank should profile its customers, thereby determining the risk according to different criteria in order to minimize and manage the risk. Risk determination when the customer is a natural and when the customer is a legal person should be carried out according to different criteria.

Criteria for initial risk determination if the customer is a natural person:

- *Sex*
- *Age*
- *Social status (based on application data)*
- *Economic power (expected inflows and outflows)*
- *Criminal record (based on Internet data or public information, World Check, Dow Jones, etc.)*
- *Psychological profile (monitoring the activities of the customer/authorized person by the bank officer)*
- *PEP*
- *Resident/non-resident*
- *Geographical areas*
- *Risky regions/countries*
- *Sanctions lists of terrorists and terrorist organizations*
- *Other blacklists.*

Based on the abovementioned criteria, bank officers are required to create an initial profile of their customer, in order to determine whether the customer is risky or not. Each of these criteria is linked to one another and gives an answer to a particular question that the bank officer asks during the profiling.

Sex and age determination gives an answer to the question about whether the customer belongs to a particular vulnerable group for which, according to these two criteria, there are suspicions it may be involved in terrorism-related activities. If we take into account statistics about the age of individuals who have committed terrorist attacks in Europe, according to which they range from 17 to 35 years old, all of which were male, in that case, customers in this group of people will be counted as risky.

Based on the data from the application form for establishing a business relation, it is determined whether the person is employed and whether he/she receives welfare, pension, etc. These data are compared with the data obtained from the analysis of the economic power of the customer, i.e., the dynamics and value of the funds that are deposited into and withdrawn from the customer's account. Then, there is a comparison of the areas or branches where the customer uses banking services. This data is important to determine whether the customer frequently changes different bank branches in order not to cause suspicion, or he/she uses banking services only from one bank officer. There upon, it is determined whether the branches the customer uses are located in areas suspected of sheltering terrorist organizations, organized crime groups, or their followers.

With the help of publicly available information through media and the Internet, it needs to be ascertained whether the customer has a criminal record in order to determine his profile. Based on the psychological profile, the bank officer should determine whether the customer performs suspicious activities in the bank, i.e., what is his physical appearance, is he nervous, afraid, does he come in the company of other persons, etc.

Also, an important aspect is whether the client is a politically exposed person or a public office holder (Member of Parliament, Director, Minister, President, etc.). These individuals enjoy greater immunity and authority in the public, and they can be abused for committing crimes.

We already mentioned that knowing the areas and countries where the customers come from should answer the question about whether the customer is a resident or comes from another high-risk country, i.e., a country that does not meet the standards for establishing a legal framework for the prevention of money laundering and terrorist financing or a state which shelters terrorist organizations, sponsors terrorist organizations, etc. Therefore, the bank should pay more attention especially if the customer wants to open a bank account in a place that is far away from his place of residence, or head office, but does not want to indicate the underlying reason for doing so. This may result in a reputational risk for the bank (if the bank does not find out that the customer comes from a region where terrorist organizations operate, or he/she is on a sanctions list of terrorists and terrorist organizations introduced by international organizations) which will also reflect on the operational and legal risk.

Finally, the bank checks the sanctions lists of terrorists and terrorist organizations adopted by international organizations, or the blacklists to which it has direct access.

Depending on the customer's risk level (low, medium, and high); the authorized persons in the bank can undertake measures for further monitoring of the customer and his/her financial activities in order to determine certain suspicious or unusual transactions that lead to money laundering and terrorist financing.

Fig. 21. *Example of Scoring Based on Different Criteria.*

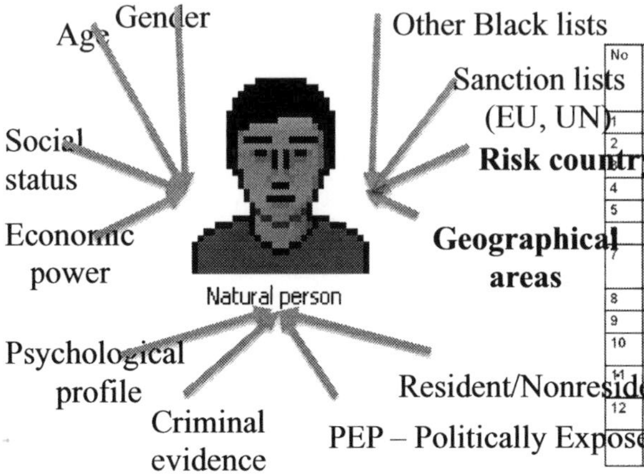

Age Gender Other Black lists Sanction lists (EU, UN) Risk country Geographical areas Social status Economic power Natural person Psychological profile Criminal evidence Resident/Nonresident PEP – Politically Exposed Person

No	Typology or criteria	Number of points (1-10)
1	Gender	5
2	Age	7
3	Social Status	6
4	Economic Profile	3
5	Psychological Profile	8
6	Criminal Evidence	8
7	PEP-Political Exposes Persons	1
8	Resident/Nonresident	6
9	Geographical Areas	8
10	Risk Country	5
11	Sanctions List (UN, EU)	5
12	Other black lists	5
	Total	67

In general, the same criteria can be used in determining the level of risk of both the legal and the natural person. In addition to the stated criteria, the bank should identify the end user of the legal person, as well as the credit rating and integrity. This will be done on the basis of the submitted documentation by the legal person or its representative. If the legal person refuses to submit the necessary documentation for determining the line of work, the authorized persons, the end owners, the necessary licenses and certificates for the line of work, and the bank may refuse the business relation.

2.1.2 Monitoring Suspicious Transactions and Submitting STR

If, according to the abovementioned criteria, the bank officers determine that the customer is of a high risk, they shall proceed to a further deeper analysis of his banking transactions in order to determine whether they are suspicious and carry out their scoring. Scoring of cash transactions, loans, exchange transactions, foreign exchange transactions, fast money transfers, etc., is also carried out. The detection of transactions which are complex and illogical, unusual for the customer and his/her line of work, i.e., transactions that deviate from the daily activities carried out with no economic or legal justification, should be an indicator (Red Flag) for suspicion and further determination of suspicion. In order to determine the suspicion of the transaction or the customer's activity, the bank needs to answer the following questions:

- The customer's risk profile
- The customer's profession and business activity
- Chronology of transactions carried out during the analysis period
- Type of transactions (cash transactions, exchange transactions, deposits, loans, fast money transfer, transfers to the home country, and international transfers)
- Determining the logical connection between the customer and the end users (family, friendly, or business connection)
- The business activity or profession of the end users (in order to determine whether the customer purchases products that can be used for making explosive devices, is preparing to depart for the war zones, etc.)
- Location of the end users of the funds (in order to determine the risky regions and states)
- Determining the source of funds
- Explaining the type and purpose of the transaction to the customer
- Verifying it with appropriate documentation
- And other questions that may be important when making the decision to submit a suspicious transactions report to the FIU.

In determining suspicious and unusual transactions and activities, the bank should focus on the transactions that are carried out on the customer's account. Namely, if the customer does not use the account according to his profile or business activity, that may be an indicator of suspicion. For example, if a 19-year-old natural person uses his deposit card for purchasing shooting range services, camping gear (boots, sleeping bags, water canisters, combat knives, etc.), airline tickets to countries that border war zones, the bank should identify these activities, recognize that the person wants to fight on a battlefield or join a terrorist organization operating in a given region, and submit a suspicious transactions report to the FIU.

In addition to the STRs, the obligated entities must submit reports on carried out transactions over 15,000 EUR and related transactions in the amount of 15,000 EUR carried out within a period of 24 hours to the FIU. Often, perpetrators of criminal acts, knowing the regulations and the threshold for reporting, decide to break down transactions to smaller amounts within a period of 24 hours.

In the figure below, we will present an example of a simulation of unusual activities on the account of a physical person-customer who went to the battlefield to join a terrorist organization.

Fig. 22. Simulation of Chronology of the Realized Transactions.

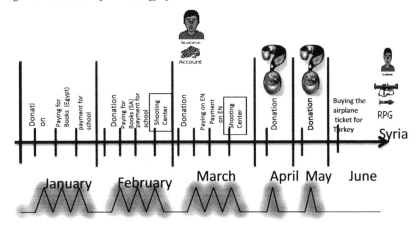

In the above simulation example, the bank is obligated to determine the unusual transactions that are carried out on the account of the natural person-customer and timely submit a suspicious transactions report to the FIU for further analysis.

Another example of determining suspicion or unusualness in the analysis of transactions is geographic regions, i.e., if transactions are transferred to regions where terrorist organizations operate, or regions around that zone, they should be subjected to analysis.

Picture 10. Transactions to/from Areas Around Conflict Zone.

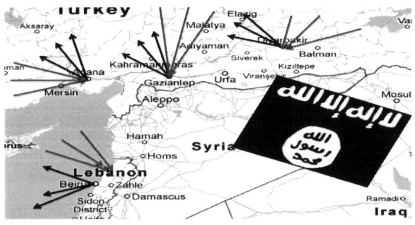

If the bank takes into account that the financial system in the ISIL-controlled area is not functional and that it is excluded from the global financial system, the transactions carried out from/to regions around the zone in which ISIL operates should be subjected to analysis. In the first chapter, we mentioned that ISIL fighter's secretly use these zones for transferring or receiving funds for the realization of their activities. According to the figure, the transactions carried out by financial institutions, located in border towns on the Turkish-Syrian border (Urfa, Gaziantep, Diyarbakir, Adana, Mersin, etc.), should be subjected to a deeper analysis that will reveal illogical or suspicious activity.

Bearing in mind that the international payment system is used by persons from different countries (having different currencies, legal regulations, etc.), banks traditionally have the role of a mediator in the payment system, i.e., in the process of carrying out payments between persons, persons and companies, and between companies. Correspondent banking, or the mediation of two or more banks in these processes, is of crucial importance in the international payment system. It is carried out using certain banking systems, such as SWIFT. SWIFT enables the exchange of standardized messages between international financial institutions concerning payments, stock trading, etc. During the analysis, bank officers should pay special attention to the bank codes in the SWIFT message. Bank codes are assigned to each bank and are composed of four individual codes: 1) Bank code; 2) Country code; 3) Location code; 4) Branch code.

Fig. 23. Example of SWIFT Code.

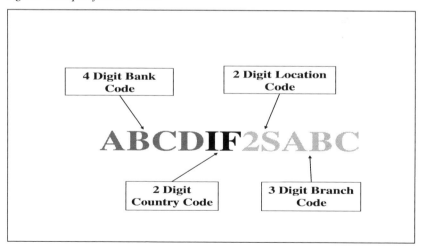

From the analysis of the SWIFT messages one can determine the location from where the money was transferred. Of particular importance are the last three digits that mark the location of the bank branch. The precise determination of the location from where the money is transferred will contribute to a better and more precise analysis to determine the degree of suspicion of a particular transaction or customer activity. As an illustration, the transaction sent by a bank branch in Brussels will not have the same weight and significance in the analysis because on a daily basis there may be many transactions that are carried out by the banks in this city. However, if, according to the SWIFT message, we find that the transaction was sent by a bank branch located in the Molenbeek municipality in Brussels, where in the past two years the Brussels police arrested many terrorists who carried out attacks in Europe, then the information is very useful. In that case, the bank should immediately conduct a thorough analysis of its customer and timely deliver a suspicious transactions report to the FIU.

Now, if we take into account that the financial system in the territory controlled by ISIL is not functional and that its members use the financial system that is in function around the controlled territory (especially the border cities in Turkey), we will accurately determine which cities in the border zone are transferring money through the last three digits of SWIFT messages.

One problem may arise when analyzing SWIFT messages. As mentioned above, each bank has a unique SWIFT message. The bank's internal policy entails whether all its branches will use a different SWIFT message when making international transfers in which the location of the branch will be precisely indicated, or the international transfers in the branches will first be directed to the bank's head office and from there under the unique SWIFT will be transferred to the final destination and end user. This will indicate that the money comes from the bank's head office and not from its branch. This is depicted in the figure below:

3. Financial Intelligence Unit

In accordance with the Convention on Laundering, Search, Seizure, and Confiscation of the Proceeds from Crime and on the Financing Terrorism of 2005 (Third EU Directive),[21] amending and updating the Strasbourg Convention

---

21 The European Parliament has so far adopted three directives but the first two did not deal with the issue of terrorist financing. The provisions of the first directive on prevention of money laundering of 1991 (Directive 91/308/EEC) were largely grounded on FATF recommendations at the time, so they did not address the issue of terrorist financing. This Directive was replaced in 2001 (Directive 2001/97/EC) by the Second

Fig. 24. Process of International Bank Transaction.

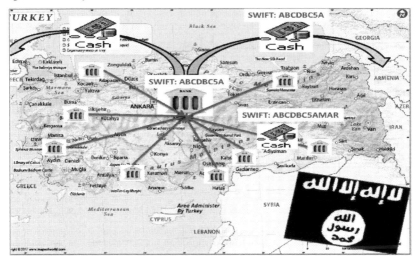

of 1990 and FATF Recommendation 26,[22] each country has an obligation to establish a FIU which will be an intermediary between the entities that are obliged to undertake measures and actions for the prevention of money laundering and terrorist financing on the one hand, and the law enforcement for prosecuting perpetrators of crimes on the other. As a result of the FATF 9 Special Recommendations on Preventing Terrorist Financing, FIU, in addition to the

---

Directive of the European Parliament, which expands the penal provisions and number of entities tasked with taking measures and actions for preventing money laundering. However, like the previous one, this directive also did not deal with terrorist financing. As a consequence of the large number of amendments and updates to the scope of the special recommendations adopted by FATF in 2003, the European Union adopted the Third Directive on the Prevention of Money Laundering and Terrorist Financing in 2005 with an implementation deadline by 2007. This directive includes provisions on terrorist financing and has expanded its application to all financial transactions that may be linked to terrorist activities.

22 In accordance with FATF Recommendation 26, each country has an obligation to establish a FIU that serves as a national center for the receiving (and, as permitted, requesting), analysis, and dissemination of STR and other information regarding potential money laundering or terrorist financing. The FIU should have access, directly or indirectly, on a timely basis to the financial, administrative, and law enforcement information that it requires to properly undertake its functions, including the analysis of STR.

competence related to the prevention of money laundering, has the competence for preventing terrorist financing. At the same time, the FIU will have the primary task of receiving, processing, analyzing, storing, and disseminating data for which there are grounds for suspicion of money laundering and terrorist financing. The purpose of the adoption of this Convention is to conduct a preventive policy that involves undertaking measures and actions before any act or crime is committed. Therefore, in accordance with this Convention, countries commit themselves to undertake legislative and other measures, both nationally and internationally, which will undoubtedly enable them to discover, find, identify, freeze, seize, and confiscate legally or illegally acquired property, or property that will be used, in whole or in part, for terrorist financing.

The FIU may be established either as an independent government agency, within the existing structure of a particular ministry, or as an independent body.[23]

To better understand the overall system and role of the FIU, we will first define the terms "competent authority" and "authorities responsible for preventing money laundering and terrorist financing." Although some of the authors (Mitsilegas) have objections to the European Directives because of the lack of precise definition of the modern FIU,[24] the First Directive gives an important contribution by laying the foundations and specifying the key differences between these terms.

The authority for preventing money laundering is mainly a body that receives and analyzes suspicious transactions and disseminates reports to the competent authorities, while the term "competent authorities" indicates the bodies as provided by law which will submit the analyzed data to the court of law, focusing on certain facts.

Article 21 of the Third EU Directive[25] gives a full definition of the FIU which describes in detail the main obligations of the FIU.

---

23 For more information, visit http://www.fatf-gafi.org (Methodology for Assessing Compliance with the FATF 40 Recommendations and the FATF 9 Special Recommendations).

24 Article 6 of the First and Second Directive provides: "Member States shall ensure that the institutions and persons subject to this Directive and their directors and employees cooperate fully with the authorities responsible for combating money laundering…," thus leaving a discretionary decision for every state to determine the method of receiving and exchanging data on suspicious transactions internally and internationally.

25 Article 21 of the Third Directive provides: "Each Member State shall establish a FIU in order effectively to combat money laundering and terrorist financing. FIU shall be established as a central national unit. It shall be responsible for receiving, analyzing and disseminating to the competent authorities, disclosures of information which concern potential money laundering, potential terrorist financing or are required by national

In this respect, Article 7, paragraph 1, item b of the UN Convention against Transnational Organized Crime stipulates that "Each State Party shall establish a FIU that will be a center responsible for receiving, analyzing and disseminating information for potential money laundering and potential terrorist financing." In addition, Article 12 of the Warsaw Convention imposes an obligation for each Member State to adopt legislative and other measures necessary for the formation of the FIU.

At the same time, according to the convention, the State has an obligation to adopt legislative or other measures that will be necessary for the FIU to have access, directly or indirectly, on a timely basis to the financial, administrative, and law enforcement information that it requires to properly undertake its functions, including the analysis of STR.

In conclusion, the FIU is a central body that has three core functions: receiving, analyzing and disseminating data to the competent state or international authorities, regardless of their organizational structure.

The first function pertaining to the receiving of data from financial and non-financial institutions, as well as from the competent state and international authorities, expresses the epithet "central authority" and determines the preventive role that the FIU has in the system. At this stage, the data are received, organized in a base and prepared for further analysis. The FIU determines the manner of receiving the necessary information (electronically or in writing), according to its possibilities and capacities.

After the necessary data are received, the next stage involves data analysis. According to the principle of induction and deduction, data are filtered in terms of their nature (separation of suspicious transactions, recognizing unusual transactions that deviate from everyday operations, detecting related transactions, etc.). On the other hand, data valorization is done within the separation itself (prioritization, determination of the limit or priority of the analysis of cash transactions, application of indicators for recognizing suspicious transactions for money laundering or terrorist financing, etc.).

In any case, it is very important to determine the degree of analysis by steps, i.e., acting in predefined and established stages within the analysis itself, due to the fact that there is a great opportunity for the financial mosaic of less significant or at first sight unrelated data to eventually result with grounds for suspicion of money laundering or terrorist financing.

---

legislation or regulation. It shall be provided with adequate resources in order to fulfil its tasks."

And FIU's third role or "house cleaning role" refers to the dissemination of data to the competent authorities for combating money laundering or terrorist financing. These data contain not only grounds for suspicion of money laundering or terrorist financing but may also contain other criminal offenses in the area of financial crime. The main purpose of the dissemination of data to the competent authorities is to conduct supervision, investigation or other specific activities (stopping the realization of a transaction, freezing of funds). This cooperation should not end here but it should continue in the further procedure until the completion of the investigation or judicial process.

3.1 Models of the FIU

The process of terrorist financing is a phenomenon that needs to be approached from several aspects. Depending on the mode of financing,[26] one of the easiest way to discover the process of terrorist financing is by tracking the money trail. For this reason, the FIU has a crucial role and is the starting point from which to collect, analyze, and disseminate data with grounds for suspicion of money laundering and terrorist financing.

In the previous point, we pointed out that international legal documents obligate member states to establish competent bodies for combating money laundering and terrorist financing. However, the success and functioning of these institutions always depend on the political support they enjoy. Namely, Article 21 of the Third EU Directive emphasizes that the FIU must have constant direct or indirect access to all necessary financial, administrative, and law enforcement information that would facilitate its functioning. In addition to this, the FATF Recommendation 30 emphasizes that each member state has an obligation to provide the necessary resources to the competent authorities involved in the fight against money laundering and terrorist financing.

According to the system for preventing money laundering and terrorist financing, the FIU can be classified by 4 operating models:

- The Administrative Model
- The Law Enforcement Model
- The Judicial Model
- The Hybrid Model

---

26 For more information, see Chapter I– Ways of transferring money for terrorist financing.

3.1.1 Administrative Model of the FIU

The administrative model of FIU is an immediate link between entities that are obliged to undertake measures and actions for the prevention of money laundering (financial and non-financial institutions) on the one hand, and the law enforcement for prosecuting perpetrators of crimes on the other. The administrative model does not offer a possibility for operational analysis of financial intelligence data, which further complicates and slows down the investigation. In reality, law enforcement should undertake operational measures in order to analyze the data from the submitted suspicious transactions reports. This operational task requires additional resources (time, operational officers, costs, etc.). On the other hand, the prevention of money laundering and terrorist financing should be prompt, timely and effective. Otherwise, if the transactions are carried out, the money is laundered, i.e., it ends up for terrorist activities, it is difficult to determine where the money ended, who was the end user and for what purposes it was used, which is contrary to the recommendations, conventions, and resolutions.

Usually, this model of FIU is formed within the ministry of finance, the national bank, or under a supervisory authority. But there are such FIUs that are formed as separate structures, independent of any ministries.

In order to better present the functioning of this type of FIU and its place in the system, we will use the following figure:

Fig. 25. Administrative Model of FIU.

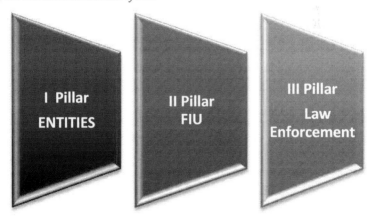

I Pillar
ENTITIES

II Pillar
FIU

III Pillar
Law
Enforcement

The basic tasks that are mainly applicable to all FIUs of an administrative type are as follows:

▷ Collecting, processing, analyzing, storing, and submitting data from entities with grounds for suspicion of money laundering and terrorist financing.

▷ Issuing an order to the entity for temporary suspending of the transaction.

▷ Cooperation with institutions from the first and third pillar.

▷ International data exchange.

▷ Control and supervision over the entities from the first pillar who are obliged to undertake measures and actions for the prevention of money laundering and terrorist financing.

The main purpose of this system is to detect a suspicious activity or transaction in the early stage, i.e., when an attempt is made to place the funds into the financial system. The first pillar entities play an important role in this detection, which on the basis of indicators for recognizing suspicious transactions and activities should recognize the suspicious activities of their customers. These indicators are produced and updated by the FIU and are submitted to all entities separately. The FIU also has the task of providing additional training for the responsible persons in the entities, which would further facilitate the way of recognizing suspicious activities and transactions.

In order to better understand the place and role of the FIU as an administrative type in the system for preventing money laundering and terrorist financing, we will explain the overall procedure.

If, on the basis of the indicators for recognizing suspicious transactions and activities, the entities of the first pillar determine some suspicion in the realization of the transactions, their purpose and economic justification, the responsible persons in the entities are obliged to submit a STR or a suspicious activities report (SAR) to the FIU.

The FIU, on the basis of its legal powers, analyzes the suspicious transaction or suspicious activity report collecting additional data from entities and competent authorities in order to determine the origin of funds and the manner of their acquisition. If necessary, the FIU may request additional information from the FIUs of other countries.

After all the data are collected, they are analyzed, and if grounds for suspicion of money laundering or terrorist financing are established, a report is prepared and submitted to the competent authority of the third pillar which is obligated to operationally check the data from the report in order to confirm the suspicion.

The data submitted by the FIU to the competent authorities cannot be used as evidence in a judicial proceeding.

This model of FIU has two advantages: first, it represents a link between the financial and non-financial sector on the one hand, and the law enforcement on the other, and second, it represents a filter between the listed entities and authorities. This means that raw data collected from the financial and non-financial sector will be analyzed; the important information will be separated from the unimportant and as a finished product with grounds for suspicion of money laundering or terrorist financing will be submitted to the investigation authorities.

Examples of the administrative model of a FIU are the US FIU (FinCEN – the Financial Crimes Enforcement Network), Slovenia's FIU (OPML – Office for Prevention of Money Laundering), France's FIU (TRAFCIN – Traitement du Renseignementet Action contre les Circuits Financiers Clandestins), the Croatian Anti-Money Laundering Department (AMLD) as part of the Ministry of Finance, etc.

The FIU of the Republic of Macedonia is a body within the Ministry of Finance and is a legal entity.

3.1.2 Law Enforcement Model of the FIU

The law enforcement model of the FIU is formed within the already existing institution, in this case the Ministry of Interior or in some states, law enforcement. Its main task is prevention, thus representing some sort of support to the competent authorities for preventing and combating money laundering and terrorist financing.

Referring to the basic definitions from the international legal documents that regulate this matter, the law enforcement model of FIU has the same powers as the administrative model, i.e., to collect, analyze, and submit reports with grounds for suspicion of money laundering and terrorist financing to the competent authorities, and in this case, the public prosecutor's office or certain departments within the law enforcement, or the customs that has competence to combat money laundering and terrorist financing.

While the administrative model has a preventive role, the main drawback of the law enforcement model of FIU is that it is more targeted to investigation than to prevention. This results in a lack of daily correspondence and working meetings between the FIU and non-financial institutions, as well as failure to carry out appropriate training and supervision of non-financial institutions by the FIU which can practically lead to a reduction in the quality and number of STRs submitted to the FIU by non-financial institutions, that further reduces the speed and quality of the analysis of these data by the FIU analysts.

In accordance with Article 35, paragraph 3 of the Third EU Directive, Member States, in this case the FIU, shall provide and timely submit feedback and statistical data on the effectiveness and quality of suspicious transactions reports, as well as the outcome of cases in their further proceeding, i.e., verdicts, which in some way emphasizes the importance of these two links in the system.

The law enforcement model is based on operational action using criminal records and available sources of national and international data exchange networks (INTERPOL and EUROPOL).[27] The processed data is sent back in a new form but is available and useful for application in the next stage of investigation.

The biggest drawback of this FIU model is the distrust by financial institutions, especially banks, since this FIU model does not require active cooperation with non-financial institutions, which in some way also interferes with the regulation of bank secrecy (Condemi & De Pasquale, 2005). Since non-financial institutions are in the private sector and their survival depends on attracting and working with customers, they are aware that every reported transaction can directly result in a specific investigation of their customer and, in a worst-case scenario, even in confirmation of the customer's illegal activities which also jeopardizes the relationship between the customer and bank.

Thus, the disadvantage of this FIU model with regard to the protection of bank secrecy will cause a wrong perception in the public that the institution has a repressive character, contrary to its original preventive role.

3.1.3 Judicial Model of the FIU

The main problem that arises in the functioning of the system for preventing money laundering and terrorist financing with this type of FIU is the lack of cooperation between the competent non-financial institutions, that are obligated to undertake measures and actions for preventing money laundering and terrorist financing and submit suspicious transactions and suspicious activities reports, and the institutions that are obligated to undertake specific measures for analysis (filtering), temporary postponing of the transactions and investigation.

The position of institutions in this type of system requires non-financial institutions to submit suspicious transactions reports directly to the FIU of a judicial model. In this case, the attorney general has no obligation to act upon all suspicious transactions reports received from non-financial institutions. The measures

---

27 There is a limit in the international data exchange, since the law enforcement model of FIU can only exchange law enforcement data, while data on accounts, transactions, and so on can be obtained only by means of international legal assistance that further complicates and slows down the cooperation between the various models of FIU in Europe and the world.

taken by this FIU model are of repressive character, that is to say, if the attorney general acts upon some STR, he/she can take measures for temporary freezing and seizure of property, or measures that limit the freedom of the suspect. The advantage of this FIU model is its position in the system. Namely, only in this system, the FIU has full control over the entire cycle from the submitting of the STR to the final outcome, that is, the verdict, the confiscation of property, or the dropping of the charge. This mode of operation leads to a reduction in the time needed for analysis, investigation, etc., making the cycles highly fast and effective with a small disadvantage which is the quality of analyzed data. In other words, they cannot be analyzed with the same quality of analysis as in the administrative model of FIU.

On the other hand, similar to the law enforcement model of FIU, the position of this FIU model can directly affect the cooperation between non-financial institutions and the FIU, i.e., there is a lack of trust, bank secrecy, trainings, etc. Also, this FIU model does not have a direct access to domestic and international databases that would be useful for full financial analysis and for creating a financial intelligence profile for a natural or legal person.

3.1.4 Hybrid Model of the FIU

In addition to the already mentioned FIU models, countries creating a system for the prevention of money laundering and terrorist financing form a combined "hybrid" model of FIU.

This FIU model shares the positive features of the previously presented models but the most common combination is the administrative-law enforcement model. The unit's base retains the administrative model but in the internal systematization and job organization, in addition to analysts from the administrative model, there should be analysts-inspectors from the law enforcement and other institutions that are combating money laundering and terrorist financing, and that can obtain the necessary data in an easier and quicker way. The goal is to reduce the time of data analysis because sometimes due to the urgency of the procedure the basic prescribed procedure for data exchange is overlooked.

In the administrative model of FIU, data exchange is usually carried out via mail, courier, etc. and the data exchange process takes several days, further slowing the speed of the analysis.

Another important problem that arises in the mutual cooperation between FIUs is their diversity. Namely, the problem arises when data is exchanged between different models of FIU. The most common problem is when data is exchanged between the administrative and law enforcement model of FIU, since the law enforcement model of FIU provides data for investigative purposes only, and such data cannot be exchanged between two different FIU models, especially not between administrative and law enforcement models.

4. Core Functions of FIUs

The definition of FIU adopted by the Egmont Group in 1996 formalized the three core functions of the FIU, receiving, analyzing, and disseminating information, data and documents about money laundering and terrorist financing and other criminal offenses that generate proceeds. According to the definition, FIU is: "A central, national agency responsible for receiving, (and as permitted, requesting), analyzing and disseminating to the competent authorities, disclosures of financial information: (i) concerning suspected proceeds of crime and potential financing of terrorism or (ii) required by national legislation or regulation, in order to combat money laundering and terrorism financing."This also includes the revised FATF recommendations of 2003. According to Recommendation 26, "Countries should establish a FIU that serves as a national center for the receiving (and, as permitted, requesting), analysis, and dissemination of STR and other information regarding potential money laundering or terrorist financing (FATF, 2003)." The three core functions of the FIU are also mentioned in the international conventions (Palermo Convention and UN Convention against Corruption).[28]

According to the definitions, although at the beginning the three core functions of the FIU were focused only on money laundering, by revising the FATF Recommendations of 2003 the FIU functions were expanded to preventing terrorist financing, and with the revised FATF Recommendations of 2012 the functions have been expanded to other predicate offences that generate proceeds.[29]

---

28 Based on both conventions, States "shall consider the establishment of a financial intelligence unit to serve as a national centre for the collection, analysis, and dissemination of information regarding potential money-laundering" Article 7. Paragraph 1(b) United Nation Convention against Transnational Organized Crime, December 2000, Italy. Retrieved 25.01.2018.https://www.unodc.org/documents/middleeastandnorthafrica/organised-crime/UNITED_NATIONS_CONVENTION_AGAINST_TRANSNATIONAL_ORGANIZED_CRIME_AND_THE_PROTOCOLS_THERETO.pdf and Article 14, Paragraph 1(b), United Nation Convention Against Corruption, December 2003, Mexico. Retrieved 25.01.2018.https://www.unodc.org/documents/brussels/UN_Convention_Against_Corruption.pdf.

29 "Countries should establish a FIU that serves as a national center for the receipt and analysis of: (a) suspicious transaction reports; and (b) other information relevant to

4.1 Receiving and Analyzing Suspicious Transactions Reports on Money Laundering and Terrorist Financing

By definition, the FIU is a central body in the system for preventing money laundering and terrorist financing that is responsible for receiving, analyzing, and disseminating data on suspicious transactions and activities to the competent investigation authorities for further investigation. The FIU may receive suspicious transactions reports from: 1) The obligated entities; 2) Data from other FIUs; 3) Data from other state bodies.

The number of reports received may vary from period to period and from country to country. The number of reports may be extremely large for the FIU to be able to analyze them all in a timely manner. In that case, the FIU has the right to prioritize the reports based on the degree of their suspicion and to act upon them from high to low priority. The reports which will not be analyzed can be stored in a database that will later serve for strategic analysis, or for linking them with previously analyzed cases.

The analytical work is a core function of almost all FIUs. For successful analytical work, the FIU should have access to different databases and other sources of information. The analysis carried out by the FIU can be tactical and strategic.

4.2 Tactical Analysis

Tactical analysis is closely related to and is in direct correlation with the quantity and quality of the collected data for a particular suspicious transactions report. Therefore, the FIU should have access to various databases that will enable fast and timely access to certain data and information necessary for the analysis of the suspicious transactions report. Through tactical analysis, the analyst tries to find a connection between suspicious transactions, legal and natural persons involved in their realization, criminal or terrorist groups and organizations, and predicate crimes.

Knowledge, direct access to all necessary databases and access to publicly available information are required for a quality and prompt processing of the suspicious transactions report. The necessary databases to which FIU should have access are the following:

---

money laundering, associated predicate offences and terrorist financing, and for the dissemination of the results of that analysis.", Recommendation 29. FATF 40 Recommendation, February 2012. Retrieved 25.01.2018 http://www.fatf-gafi.org/media/fatf/documents/recommendations/pdfs/FATF_Recommendations.pdf.

- <u>FIU's database</u> – As previously mentioned, the obligated entities must submit suspicious transactions reports, transactions over 15,000 EUR and related transactions in the amount of 15,000 EUR and more. All this data should be stored in a separate database (electronic) that will be used for the current analytical work of the FIU. The internal database of the FIU includes all data and requests submitted by other competent authorities as well as by foreign FIUs. In addition to these data, the Customs Administration is also obliged to report to the FIU the entering and exiting of money or physically transferable assets for payment of over 10,000 EUR. All these data, as well as data from previously performed analyzes, should be stored in the internal database of the FIU that will serve as a source of information for the current analysis of a particular case.

- <u>Access to databases of other state institutions</u> – The dynamics and speed of both money laundering and terrorist financing require a quick response through their timely detection and prevention. During the financial analysis, the FIU needs direct and quick access to databases and registers of other relevant institutions through which it will provide quality and necessary data. For that purpose, the FIU should have direct electronic access to databases and registers that will be regulated by law or a memorandum between the FIU and other institutions. Any changes in the databases and registers should be delivered in real time to the FIU via web services and an interoperability system. Generally, FIU needs direct electronic access to the following databases:

  - *Database of criminal records* – which will provide data on the involvement of natural or legal persons in criminal activities.

  - *Database of birth certificates* – which will provide data for the members of the immediate and extended family of the natural person that is subject to analysis.

  - *Database of the Register of Motor Vehicles* – which will provide data on the number and type of vehicles that persons own.

  - *Database of the Register of Watercrafts* (boat, motorboat, yachts, cruisers, etc.) – which will provide data on the number and type of watercrafts that persons own.

  - *Database of the Register of Aircrafts* (helicopters, airplanes, unmanned aerial vehicles, etc.) – which will provide data on the number and type of aircrafts that persons own.

  - *Access to the database of the number of bank accounts* – which will provide data on the number and type of accounts owned by a natural or legal person, data on the bank in which they are opened, the time of their opening or closing, authorized persons, etc.

- *Access to the register of employment* – which will provide data on the employment status of a natural person as well as his/her employment history. For a legal person, data will be provided on which and how many persons are employed there.

- *Access to the Real Estate Register* – which will provide data on the number and type of real estates that are owned by a particular natural or legal person.

- *Access to the Company register* – which will provide data on the ownership of the legal entity, date of opening, headquarters, amount of invested funds, subsidiaries, history of the ownership structure, and other necessary data.

- *Access to the tax database* – which will provide data on the recorded incomes and expenditures reported by a natural or legal person, as well as the outcomes of their auditing.

- *Access to the Securities Register* – which will provide data on the ownership of securities.

- *Other databases and registers that may be necessary for the purposes of financial analysis.*

- Access to publicly available databases – Access to publicly available databases and information published in the media, newspapers, web portals or social networks is the third condition for a successful financial analysis. In practice, the access to some of these publicly available data is free but for others it must be paid. The most commonly used are:
  - World Check database
  - Data from public media and newspapers
  - Data from internet and social networks
  - Dow Jones database
  - List of terrorists and terrorist organizations (UN, EU, OFAC)
  - Dun & Bradstreet database

All of the above data are necessary for quality and fast financial analysis. These data are used for the profiling of natural or legal persons, determining their line of work in the past, the manner of acquiring all of their material possessions, the basis and logic for the financial transactions they carry out, determining suspicion or unusualness in them as well as a basis for monitoring future activities. The outcome of the financial analysis should dispel any suspicion or result in dissemination of data to the investigating authorities for their further analysis.

Fig. 26. FIU Information Flow.

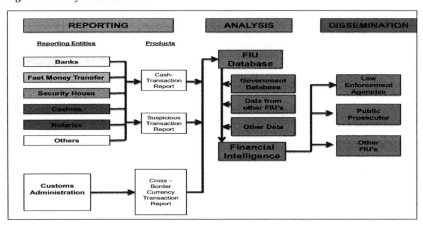

4.3 Strategic Analysis

Contrary to the tactical analysis focused on the financial analysis of a particular case of money laundering or terrorist financing, the strategic analysis is focused on determining an event that happened, happens, or will happen in a given period of time. Strategic analysis will help the FIU in the preparation of strategic plans for its future work and focus, i.e., whether certain customers, geographical areas, sectors, products, and activities should be subject to further analysis and appropriate measures and actions to overcome, eliminate, or prevent them. To that end, all available data of the FIU are used.

From the aspect of the fight against terrorist financing, strategic analysis can help us in determining increased or reduced frequency of carried out transactions from/to risky regions and countries where a terrorist organization operates or that are affected by armed conflicts, or regions and states around them. An example of a strategic analysis can be the increased frequency of transactions from/to border towns on the Turkish-Syrian border (Diyarbakir, Gaziantep, Adana, etc.). The subject of the analysis will be to determine the cause, frequency of transactions, used sector (bank, fast money transfer service providers), customers and end users of the funds, their possible connection with terrorist activities, etc. The strategic analysis should produce appropriate measures and actions that all financial institutions and state authorities should undertake in order to determine the ultimate purpose of transactions from/to that region. They can designate the region as "high risk" placing a ban on the transfers from/to this region.

144

4.4 Dissemination of Reports

Timely dissemination of data on suspicious transactions and activities arising from the conducted financial analysis is of crucial importance in the process of prevention of money laundering or terrorist financing. The ability of the FIU to quickly analyze and disseminate data on suspicious transactions and activities to the competent authorities on a national level, as well as to send information to foreign FIUs is the main reason for its success. It practically measures the success of the national AML/CTF system.

The dissemination of data to the competent institutions may be on a national and international level. At the national level, the FIU disseminates suspicious transactions reports to the competent authorities (law enforcement or prosecutor's office) for the purpose of investigating and prosecuting. The legal framework in the country prescribes to which institution the report will be submitted. In countries where the FIU is of an administrative type, the financial analysis conducted by the FIU is an intelligence work and contains grounds for suspicion of money laundering and terrorist financing. In those cases, the FIU submits a report to the law enforcement that has the authority to conduct further investigation. However, in cases where the FIU is of a law enforcement-administrative type, the report is submitted to the public prosecutor's office in order to file a criminal charge. Therefore, depending on the jurisdiction and type of FIU (law enforcement, and judicial), they have the legal capacity to initiate investigations and file charges for cases related to money laundering or terrorist financing.

Taking into account the international character of both money laundering and terrorist financing processes, there is a need for international cooperation between different countries. The legal basis for establishing this cooperation is bilateral or multilateral agreements or memoranda of cooperation. The international cooperation between FIUs can be based on the principle: 1) submitting a request/response and 2) sending spontaneous information from a conducted analysis.

During the financial analysis of money laundering and terrorist financing cases by the FIU, there may arise a need to request data from another FIU that are necessary for the outcome of the analysis. For this purpose, the FIU submits a data request to another FIU. The exchange of requests and responses is done in accordance with the established standards of the EGMONT Group,[30] through a separate channel called Egmont Security Web Site. This direct line is also used for exchanging information related to various types of statistics, typologies,

---

30 Egmont Group – an informal group of all FIUs worldwide that meet the basic standards for the prevention of money laundering and terrorist financing.

practical cases, trainings and workshops, etc. In the EU, a decentralized and sophisticated computer network "FIU.net" has been established supporting FIUs in their fight against money laundering and the financing of terrorism.[31] Through the security channel of FIU.net, FIUs, including EUROPOL, can exchange data.

4.5 Postponing and Freezing Suspicious Transactions

With the implementation of the preventive policy, the prevention of money laundering and terrorist financing should be timely, in the early stage, i.e., when the proceeds of crime or the funds for financing terrorist activities are placed into the financial sector. At this stage, financial institutions should have an appropriate legal capacity to recognize suspicious transactions and temporarily suspend them. In accordance with international standards, the FIU has no power to directly block funds. According to these standards, countries should adopt legislative and other measures that will enable timely postponing and freezing of suspicious transactions, with an obligation to conduct an analysis and confirm the suspicion.[32] The FATF Recommendation 4 states that "countries should adopt appropriate legislative measures that will allow proceeds of crime to be confiscated" (FATF, 2012).

Recognizing suspicious transactions is a complex matter. Being from the private sector, financial institutions are obligated to carry out or suspend a particular transaction. If they suspend the transaction, there is a possibility to lose the customer and hence the profit, and if they carry out the transaction, there is a possibility to be involved in the process of money laundering or terrorist financing.

In this stage, the cooperation between the FIU and financial institutions is extremely important. Namely, the FIU produces indicators for recognizing suspicious transactions for each entity individually which are submitted to them in order to facilitate and simplify the recognition and separation of suspicious from unsuspicious transactions, as well as recognizing the suspicious activities of customers.

31 Council Decision "Concerning arrangements for cooperation between financial intelligence units of the Member States in respect of exchanging information" 2000/642/JHA, Published in Official Journal of the European Communities No. L 271/4 from 24.10.2000. Retrieved 31.01.2018. http://eur-lex.europa.eu/legal-content/EN/TXT/PDF/?uri=CELEX:32000D0642&from=EN.

32 See [Strasbourg] Convention on Laundering, Search, Seizure and Confiscation of the Proceeds from Crime, Article 3; United Nations Convention against Transnational Organized Crime, Article 12; and International Convention for the Suppression of the Financing of Terrorism, Article 8.

A suspicious transaction may also be suspended after the entity has submitted a STR to the FIU. Namely, if during the financial analysis, the FIU determines that the carrying out of a particular transaction is a process of money laundering or terrorist financing, the FIU can submit a request to the bank to postpone the transaction temporarily. Globally, the time period for postponing the transaction is different from jurisdiction to jurisdiction. For example, in the Republic of Macedonia, the Financial Intelligence Office has legal power to submit a request for postponing the transaction for a maximum of 72 hours.[33] During this period, the Office submits a request to the competent public prosecutor for proposal on determining provisional measures. The request shall include data on the crime, facts, and circumstances that justify the need for the provisional measure, data on the natural or legal person that performs the transaction, the entity where the transaction is performed and the amount of the money. The public prosecutor shall review the request and if determines that it is reasonable, without any delay, no longer than 24 hours of the receiving of the request, he/she submits a proposal for determining provisional measures to the judge of the competent court. The judge of the competent court shall be obliged within 24 hours to adopt a decision for implementation of the provisional measures or deny the proposal of the public prosecutor.[34]

4.6 Monitoring of Customer's Business Relations

The monitoring of customer's business relations (especially the ones that the bank has categorized with a high degree of risk during a business relation) is essential in order to determine whether the customer is involved in a process of money laundering or terrorist financing. FATF Recommendation 10 entails that "financial institutions should be required to undertake CDD measures when":

(i) Establishing business relations;
(ii) Carrying out occasional transactions: (i) above the applicable designated threshold (USD/EUR 15,000); or (ii) that are wire transfers in the circumstances covered by the Interpretive Note to Recommendation 16;
(iii) There is a suspicion of money laundering or terrorist financing; or
(iv) The financial institution has doubts about the veracity or adequacy of previously obtained customer identification data" (FATF, 2012).

---

33 See Law on Prevention of Money Laundering and Financing of Terrorism (Official Gazette of RM No. 130/2014).
34 Ibid.

FIUs should have legal power to submit an order for monitoring business relations to the obligated entities if they determine that for a particular transaction or person there is a basis for suspicion of money laundering or terrorist financing. The order obligates entities to monitor all transactions or activities of the persons listed in the order. Unless otherwise specified in the order, the obligated entity is required to inform the FIU before a transaction or activity is conducted. The monitoring of the business relation usually lasts 3 months, and for justified reasons this measure can be extended for one month but not more than six months in total.[35]

---

35 See: Law on Prevention of Money Laundering and Financing of Terrorism (Official Gazette of RM, 130/2014) article 82, AML/CTF Law (Official Gazette of RS, 113/2017) article 76, AML/CTF Law (Official Gazette of MN, 33/2014) article 63.

List of Figures

List of Tables

List of Photos

Bibliography

1999/352/EC. (1999). *Commission Decision of 28 April 1999 Establishing the European Anti-fraud Office (OLAF).* Retrieved 05 15, 2017, from EUR-Lex Access to European Union Law: http://eur-lex.europa.eu/LexUriServ/LexU riServ.do?uri=OJ:L:1999:136:0020:0022:EN:PDF

2000/642/JHA. (2000). *Council Decision of 17 October 2000 Concerning Arrangements for Cooperation Between Financial Intelligence Units of the Member States in Respect of Exchanging Information.* Retrieved 05 15, 2017, from EUR-Lex Access to European Union Law: http://eur-lex.europa.eu/legal-content/EN/TXT/PDF/?uri=CELEX:32000D0642&from=EN

2001/500/JHA. (2001). *Council Framework Decision of 26 June 2001 on Money Laundering, the Identification, Tracing, Freezing, Seizing and Confiscation of Instrumentalities and the Proceeds of Crime.* Retrieved 05 10, 2017, from EUR-Lex Access to European Union Law: http://eur-lex.europa.eu/legal-content/GA/TXT/?uri=CELEX:32001F0500

2001/930/CFSP. (2001). *Council Common Position of 27 December 2001 on Combatting Terrorism.* Retrieved 05 20, 2017, from EUR-Lex Access to European UnionLaw:http://eur-lex.europa.eu/legal-content/EN/TXT/PDF/?uri=CELEX:32001E0930&from=EN

2001/931/CFSP. (2001). *Council Common Position of 27 December 2001 on the Application of Specific Measures to Combat Terrorism.* Retrieved 05 25, 2017, from EUR-Lex Access to the European Union Law: http://eur-lex.europa.eu/LexUriServ/LexUriServ.do?uri=OJ:L:2001:344:0093:0096:EN:PDF

2001/97/EC. (2001). *Directive 2001/97/EC of the European Parliament and of the Council of 4 December 2001.* Retrieved 05 15, 2017, from EUR-Lex Access to European Law: http://eur-lex.europa.eu/resource.html?uri=cellar:57ce32a4-2d5b-48f6-adb0-c1c4c7f7a192.0004.02/DOC_1&format=PDF

2005/60/EC. (2005). *Directive 2005/60/EC of the European Parliament and of the Council of 26 October 2005 on the Prevention of the Use of the Financial System for the Purpose of Money Laundering and Terrorist Financing.* Retrieved 05 30, 2017, from EUR-Lex Access to European Union Law: http://eur-lex.europa.eu/LexUriServ/LexUriServ.do?uri=OJ:L:2005:309:0015:0036:en:PDF

91/308/EEC. (1991). *Council Directive 91/308/EEC of 10 June 1991 on Prevention of the Use of the Financial System for the Purpose of Money Laundering.* Retrieved 05 10, 2017, from EUR-Lex Access to European Union Law. URL: http://eur-lex.europa.eu/legal-content/EN/TXT/HTML/?uri=LEGISSUM:l24016&from=ENG

AAOIFI. (2017). *Shari'a Standards*. Retrieved 05 01, 2017, from The Accounting and Auditing Organization for Islamic Financial Institutions: http://aaoifi.com/standard/shariah-standards/?lang=en

Aaron, Z. Y. (2014, June). *The War Between ISIS and Al-Qaeda for Supremacy of the Global Jihadist Movement*. Retrieved 01 09, 2018, from washingtoninstitute.org: http://www.washingtoninstitute.org/uploads/Documents/pubs/Research Note_20_Zelin.pdf

Adams, A. (1987). The Financing of Terror. In P. W. Stewards, *Contemporary Research of Terrorism*. Aberdeen: Aberdeen University Press.

Akgun, M. (2017, January 23). *Bize Gore Teror Neyse Uyusturucu da o Olmali*. Retrieved 01 26, 2017, from ilkhaber.net: http://www.ilkhaber.net/siyaset/bize-gore-teror-neyse-uyusturucu-da-o-olmali-h8920.html

Alexandra, W. (2017, October 21). *Donald Trump Says, 'end of Isis caliphate is in sight' After De facto Capital of Raqqa Recaptured*. Retrieved 08.01.2018, from Independent.co.uk: http://www.independent.co.uk/news/world/americas/us-politics/isis-donald-trump-raqqa-recaptured-syria-end-of-caliphate-in-sight-terror-attacks-threat-latest-a8013196.html

Alharbi, A. (2015, June). Development of the Islamic Banking System. *Journal of Islamic Banking and Finance*, Vol. 3, No. 1, 12–25.

Aliyu, A. A., & Tasmin, R. B. HJ. (2012). The Impact of Information and Communication Technology on Bank's, Performance and Customer Service Delivery in the Banking Industry. *International Journal of Latest Trends in Finance & Economic Science*, Vol. 2, No. 1. P. 80–90.

Altunok, T., & Denizer, O. (2009). Terörizmin Yasal Olmayan Finans Kaynakları. In H. Cakmak & T. Altunok, *Terörizmin Finansmanı ve Ekonomisi* (pp. 95–116). Baris Platin Ankara.

Anderson, S. (1994, February 1). *Making a Killing: The High Cost of Peace in Northern Ireland*. Retrieved 10 17, 2017, from highbeam.com:https://www.highbeam.com/doc/1G1-14765886.html

Anissed, E. V. (2013). Hezbollah: from a Terrorist to a Political Party-Social Work as a Key to Politics. In E. V. Anissed, D. A. Van & M. R. Rudolph, *From Terrorism to Politics* (pp. 33–34).Hampshire, Ashgate Publishing Limited.

APG. (2017). *Asia Pasific Group on Money Laundering*. Retrieved 07 10, 2017, from Asia Pacific Group on Money Laundering: http://www.apgml.org/

Al-Zarqawi, A. M. (2004, October 18). *Zarqawi's Pledge of Allegiance to Al-Qaeda: From Mu'Asker Al Battar*. Retrieved: 01.09,2018, from jamestown.org (Jamestown Foundation): https://jamestown.org/program/zarqawis-pledge-of-allegiance-to-al-qaeda-from-muasker-al-battar-issue-21-2/

Barnard, A. (2014, January 3). *Mystery in Hezbollah Operatives Life and Death.* Retrieved 01 08, 2018, from *The New York Times*:https://www.nytimes. com/2014/01/04/world/middleeast/mystery-in-hezbollah-operatives-life-and-death.html

Basel Committee for Banking Supervision. (2000). *Electronic Banking Group Initiatives and White Papers.* Basel: Basel Committee for Banking Supervision.

Bennet, M. (2015, September 28). *11 Types of Credit Card Fraud.* Retrieved 10 16, 2017, from Consumer Protect: https://www.consumerprotect.com/11-types-of-credit-card-fraud/

Biersteker,T. J., & Eckert, S. (2008a). Introduction: The Challenge of Terrorist Financing. In T. J. Biersteker & S. E. Eckert, *Countering in the Financing of Terrorism* (pp. 1–17). New York: Routledge.

Biersteker, T. J., & Eckert, S. E. (2008b). Terrorist Financing Mechanism and Policy Delemmas. In T. J. Eckert, *Countering the Financing of Terrorism* (p. 25). New York: Routledge.

Bilefsky, D. (2014, December 5). *Charity in France is Accused of Being a Front for Financing Terrorism in Syria.* Retrieved 12.01.2018, from nytimes.com: https://www.nytimes.com/2014/12/05/world/charity-in-france-is-accused-of-being-a-front-for-financing-terrorism-in-syria.html

Brisard, J.-C. (2002, December 19). *Terrorism Financing: Roots and Trends of Saudi Terrorism Financing.* Retrieved 03 15, 2017, from The Investigative Project on Terrorism: http://www.investigativeproject.org/documents/testimony/22.pdf

BRITEL. (2015, August 22). *Hizbullah's Learning Curve: Deadly Experience.* Retrieved 0109, 2018, from The Economist: https://www.economist.com/news/middle-east-and-africa/21661826-costly-valuable-lessons-guerrilla-army-once-fought

Brooke, S. (2017, November 1). *Timeline of Recent Terror Attacks Against the West.* Retrieved 15.01.2018, from foxnews.com: http://www.foxnews.com/world/2017/11/01/timeline-recent-terror-attacks-against-west.html

Nazemroaya, M. (2006, November 18). Plans for Redrawing the Middle East: The Project for a "New Middle East". *Global Research.* Retrieved 25.10.2017 from Centre for Research on Globalization GLOBAL RESEARCH: https://www.globalresearch.ca/plans-for-redrawing-the-middle-east-the-project-for-a-new-middle-east/3882

CFATF. (2017). *Caribbean Financial Action Task Force.* Retrieved 07 20, 2017, from Carribean Financial Action Task Force: https://www.cfatf-gafic.org/

Condemi, M., & De Pasquale, F. (2005). *International Profiles of the Activity to Prevent and Combat Money Laundering.* Roma: Ufficio Italiano dei Cambi, Roma.

Council, A. F. (2014). *The World Almanac of Islamism: 2014*. Rowman & Littlefield, Lanham, Maryland, 2014.

Daniel, B. & Jeremy, S. (2014). Be Afraid, Be A Little Afraid: The Threat of Terrorism from Western Foreign Fighters in Syria and Iraq. Policy Paper No. 34, Brookings, Washington, 7.

Drezner, D. W. (2012, February 9). *Contribution to "What Should the United States Do About Syria? A TNR Symposium"*. Retrieved 13.02. 2018, from newrepublic.com: https://newrepublic.com/article/100565/syria-symposium-assad-arab-league-intervention.

EAG. (2017). *Euroasian Group of Combatting Money Laundering and Financing Terrorism*. Retrieved 07 20, 2017, from Euroasian Group of Combatting Money Laundering and Financing Terrorism: http://www.eurasiangroup.org/

EC No 2580/2001. (2001). *Regulation (EC) No 2580/2001 Specific Restrictive Measures Directed Against Certain Persons and Entities with a View to Combating Terrorism*. Retrieved 05 20, 2017, from EUR-Lex Access to European Union Law: http://eur-lex.europa.eu/legal-content/EN/TXT/PDF/?uri=CELEX: 32001R2580&from=EN

EC No 881/2002. (2002). *Council Regulation (EC) No 881/2002 Of 27 May 2002 Imposing Certain Specific Restrictive Measures Directed Against Certain Persons and Entities Associated with Usama bin Laden, the Al-Qaida Network and the Taliban, and Repealing Council Regulation (EC) No 467/2001 Prohibiting the Export of Certain Goods and Services to Afghanistan, Strengthening the Flight Ban and Extending the Freeze of Funds and Other Financial Resources in Respect of the Taliban of Afghanistan*. Retrieved 05 20, 2017, from EUR-Lex Access to European Union Law: http://eur-lex.europa.eu/legal-content/EN/TXT/PDF/?uri=CELEX:32002R0881&from=EN

Eder, E. (1998). Definition und Gebrauch des Begriffes "Strategie". *Osterreichische Militaerische Zeitshrift*, Vol. 36., p. 121–128.

Ehmed, H. (2015, August 10). İşte *PKK'nin yıllık geliri*. Retrieved 10 16, 2017, from Rudaw: http://www.rudaw.net/turkish/business/10082015

El-Badawy, E., Comerford, M., & Welby, P. (2015). *Inside the Jihadi Mind: Understanding Ideology and Propaganda*. London: Tony Blair Institute for Global Change.

el-Said, H., & Barrett, R. (2017). *Enhancing the Understanding of the Foreign Terrorist Fighters Phenomenon in Syria*. New York: United Nations Office of Counter-Terrorism.

ESAAMLG. (2017). *Euroasian Group on Combatting Money Laundering and Financing of Terrorism*. Retrieved 07 20, 2017, from Euroasian Group on Combatting Money Laundering and Financing of Terrorism: http://www.eurasian group.org/esaamlg.php

EU 2015/849. (2015). *Directive (EU) 2015/849 of the European Parliament and of the Council of 20 May 2015 on the Prevention of the Use of the Financial System for the Purposes of Money Laundering or Terrorist Financing, Amending Regulation (EU) No 648/2012 of the European Parliament and of the Council, and Repealing Directive 2005/60/EC of The European Parliament and of the Council and Commission Directive 2006/70/EC.* Retrieved 05 30, 2017, from EUR-Lex Accsess to European Union Law: http://eur-lex.europa.eu/legal-content/EN/TXT/HTML/?uri=CELEX:32015L0849&from=EN

EUROPOL. (2016). *TE-SAT 2017, EU Terrorism Situation and Trend Report 2016.* The Hague: Europol Corporate Communications.

F. Dahmoush al-Mashhour and Syrians for Democracy. (2016). *The Impact of International Coalition Operations on the Economy of Islamic State in Syria.* Deir Ezzor: JFL Observatory.

FATF. (1990). *The Forty Recommendations of the Financial Action Task Force on Money Laundering.* Retrieved 06 05, 2017, from FATF: http://www.fatf-gafi.org/media/fatf/documents/recommendations/pdfs/FATF%20Recommendations%201990.pdf

FATF. (2001). *FATF IX Special Recommendations.* Retrieved 06 15, 2017, from FATF: http://www.fatf-gafi.org/media/fatf/documents/reports/FATF%20Standards%20-%20IX%20Special%20Recommendations%20and%20IN%20rc.pdf

FATF. (2003). *The Forty Recommendation.* France: FATF Secretariat.

FATF. (2012). *International Standards on Combatting Money Laundering and the Financing of Terrorism and Proliferation: The FATF Recommendations.* Retrieved 06 10, 2017, from FATF: http://www.fatf-gafi.org/media/fatf/documents/recommendations/pdfs/FATF_Recommendations.pdf

FATF. (2015). *Financing of the Terrorist Organization Islamic State in Iraq and the Levant.* Paris: FATF.

FATF-GIABA-GABAC. (2016). *Terrorist Financing in West and Central Africa.* Paris: FATF.

Federal Financial Institution Examination Council. (2003, August). *FFIEC Information Technology Examination Handbook (IT Examination Handbook – e-Banking).* Retrieved 02 28, 2018, from FFIEC: https://ithandbook.ffiec.gov/media/274777/ffiec_itbooklet_e-banking.pdf

Fishman, B. (2013, November 26). *Syria Proving More Fertile than Iraq to Al-Qaeda's Operations.* Retrieved 27.08.2017, from ctc.usma.edu: https://www.ctc.usma.edu/posts/syria-proving-more-fertile-than-iraq-to-al-qaidas-operations

G-7 Summit. (1989). *Economic Declaration Paris, July 16, 1989.* Retrieved 06 15, 2017, from G7 Information Centre: http://www.g8.utoronto.ca/summit/1989paris/communique/index.html#drugs

GAFILAT. (2017). *The Financial Action Task Force of Latin America*. Retrieved 07 20, 2017, from The Financial Action Task Force of Latin America: http://www.gafilat.org/

Geneva Academy of International Humanitarian Law and Human Rights. (2014). *Foreign Fighters under International Law*. Geneva: Geneva Academy of International Humanitarian Law and Human Rights.

Georgieva-Trajkovska, O. (2009). Elektronsko bankarstvo-poim i rizici. *Godisen Zbornik Volume 1, Ekonomski Fakultet, Univerztet "Goce Delcev" Stip*, 162–172.

GIABA. (2017). *Intergovenmental Action Group Against Money Laundering in West Africa*. Retrieved 07 20, 2017, from Intergovenmental Action Group Against Money Laundering in West Africa: http://www.giaba.org/

Glanville, R. (2013, June 3). *Eleven Types of Credit Card Fraud*. Retrieved 12 12, 2017, from Scamsinc.com: http://scamsinc.com/2013/06/03/eleven-types-of-credit-card-fraud/

Grurof, E. (1996). Perenjeto pari (germanska pravna regulativa) i izbrani slucai na investiranje vo nedviznosti, somnitelni finansiski transakcii i drugo vo vrska so perenjeto pari. Bezbednost Volume.1, 415–426.

Gunter, M. (1991). Transnational Sources of Support for the Kurdish Insurgency in Turkey. The Journal of Conflict Studies, Vol. 11, No.2, 7–29.

Haidamous, L. S. (2015, February 16). *Lebanon's Hezbollah Acknowledges Battling the Islamic State in Iraq*. Retrieved 01 09, 2018, from *The Washington Post*: https://www.washingtonpost.com/world/middle_east/lebanons-hezbollah-acknowledges-battling-the-islamic-state-in-iraq/2015/02/16/4448b21a-b619-11e4-bc30-a4e75503948a_story.html?utm_term=.fd24c40ad929

Harriet, A. (2017, June 6). *London Bridge Attack: Everything We Know*. Retrieved 09.01.2018, from telegraph.co.uk: http://www.telegraph.co.uk/news/2017/06/03/london-bridge-everything-know-far/

Harris, P., Burhan, W., & Connolly, K. (2002, April 21). *Al-Qaeda's Bombers used Britain to Plot Slaughter*. Retrieved 2017, from The Guardian.com: https://www.theguardian.com/world/2002/apr/21/terrorism.religion

Haselmann, R., & Vig, V. (2007, June 21). *The Differential of Bank Liberalization*. Retrieved 11 23, 2017, from bundesbank.de: https://www.bundesbank.de/Redaktion/EN/Downloads/Bundesbank/Research_Centre/Conferences/2007/2007_06_21_eltville_01_haselmann_vig_paper.pdf?__blob=publicationFile

Hinnant, L. (2016, December 6). *The Syrian Bishop who Saved 226 Christian Hostages from Isis*. Retrieved 01 16, 2018, from independent.co.uk:http://www.independent.co.uk/news/world/middle-east/syrian-bishop-mar-afram-athneil-saved-226-christian-hostages-isis-a7458376.html

Hoffman, B. (1998). *Inside Terrorism*. Columbia University Press New York.

Holly, Y., & Andone, D. (2017, November 1). *Who is New York Terror Suspect Sayfullo Saipov.* Retrieved 2018, from edition.cnn.com: http://edition.cnn.com/2017/11/01/us/sayfullo-saipov-new-york-attack/index.html

Howcraft, J. (2016). *The Strategy and Tactics of Terrorism.* In J. K. Mullins, *Combating Transnational Terrorism* (p. 33). Bulgaria: Procon Ltd.

Hurriyet. (2010, November 2). *Yunanistan Lavrion Multeci Kampi'ni kapatiyor.* Retrieved 2017, from huriyet.com.tr: http://www.hurriyet.com.tr/yunanistan-lavrion-multeci-kampini-kapatiyor-16195864

Inspire Magazine. (2016, November). *The 9/17 Operations.* Retrieved from *Inspire Magazine*: https://azelin.files.wordpress.com/2016/11/inspiremagazine-16.pdf

Institute for Economics & Peace. (2015). *Global Terrorism Index 2015.* Sydney: Institute for Economics & Peace.

Institute for Economics & Peace. (2017). *Global Terrorism Index 2017.* Sydney: Institute for Economics & Peace.

Intelligence, U. S. (2006). *Postwar Findings About Iraq's WMD Programs and Links to Terrorism and How they Compare with Prewar Assessments.* Washington: US Senate Select Committee. Retrieved from https://www.intelligence.senate.gov/sites/default/files/publications/109331.pdf.

Jazeera, A. (2014, February 5). *Hezbollah Suspected in Bulgaria Bus Bombing.* Retrieved 01 08, 2018, from Al Jazeera: https://www.aljazeera.com/news/europe/2013/02/20132515350158754.html

John, H., & Max, T. (2007, December 21). *Playing the Green Card – Financing the Provisional IRA: Part 1.* Retrieved 12 21, 2017, from tandfonline.com: https://www.tandfonline.com/doi/abs/10.1080/09546559908427502

Karapınar, A. (2003). *Özel Finans Kurumları ve Muhasebe Uygulaması.* Ankara: Gazi Kitapevi.

Kareem, S. (2017, January 20). *ISIS Destroys tetrapylon monument in Palmyra.* Retrieved 01 17, 2018, from The Guardian.com:https://www.theguardian.com/world/2017/jan/20/isis-destroys-tetrapylon-monument-palmyra-syria

Kemal, M. (2016, November 2). *Multeci kampi PKK kampi'ne donutty.* Retrieved 2017, from timeturk: http://www.timeturk.com/multeci-kampi-pkk-kampina-donustu/haber-357900

Kılıç, B. (2011, May 12). *Ladin'in Babası Baba Bush'un Suç Ortağıydı.* Retrieved 03 20, 2017, from Yeniçağ: http://www.yenicaggazetesi.com.tr/ladinin-babasi-baba-bushun-suc-ortagiydi-18225yy.htm

Kohlmann, E. F. (2005). *Al-Qaidin džihad u Europi: Afganistansko-bosanska mreža.* Zagreb: Naklada Ljevak d.o.o.

KOM. (2014). *Kaçakçılık ve Organize Suçlarla Mücadele 2013 Raporu*. Ankara: KOM.

Koroglu, U. (2012, December 20). *Komşuda DHKP-C'nin 3 kampı var*. Retrieved 2017, from sabah.com.tr: http://www.sabah.com.tr/gundem/2012/12/20/komsuda-dhkpcnin-3-kampi-var

Lawrence, J. (2014, July 2). *Iraq Crisis: Could an ISIS Caliphate Ever Dovern the Entire Muslim World?* Retrieved 01 09, 2018, from abc.net.au: http://www.abc.net.au/news/2014-07-02/could-an-isis-caliphate-ever-govern-the-muslim-world/5559806

Levitt, T. (1983). The Globalization of Markets. *Harvard Business Review*, Volume 1

Libnan, Y. (2015, June 16). *Hezbollah Claims Capturing More Territory from ISIS in Qalamoun*. Retrieved 01 18, 2018, from yalibnan.com: http://yalibnan.com/2015/06/16/hezbollah-claims-capturing-more-territory-from-isis-in-qalamoun/

Local, S. (2012, June 29). *Glasgow Airport Attack: Timeline of a Terrorist Act*. Retrieved 2017, from stv.tv: https://stv.tv/news/west-central/107856-glasgow-airport-terror-attack-timeline-the-planning-of-a-massacre/

Loulla, M., & Eleftheriou, S. (2015, December 9). *Global Terrorism Index: Map Show where 42 Different Militant Groups have Pledged Support to ISIS*. Retrieved 01 10, 2018, from independent.co.uk: http://www.independent.co.uk/news/world/middle-east/global-terrorism-index-the-map-that-shows-where-42-different-militant-groups-have-pledged-support-to-a6767051.html

Maltz, D. S. (2017, June 8). *Attacking Hezbollah's Financial Network: Policy Options*. Retrieved 01 01, 2018, from United States House of Represenatives house Committee of Foreign Affairs:http://docs.house.gov/meetings/FA/FA00/20170608/106094/HHRG-115-FA00-Wstate-MaltzD-20170608.pdf

Mandhai, S. (2014, July 7). *Muslim Leaders Reject Baghdadi's Caliphate*. Retrieved 01 09, 2018, from aljazeera.com:http://www.aljazeera.com/news/middleeast/2014/07/muslim-leaders-reject-baghdadi-caliphate-20147744058773906.html

Mannes, A. (2003). *Profiles in Terror: The Guide to Middle East Terrorist Organization*. Rowman & Littlefield: Lanham, Maryland

Mannes, A. (2004). *Profiles in Terror*. Oxford: Rowman & Littlefield Publishers.

Martin, W. (2016, December 2). *One Chart Shows How Little its Costs Terrorist Groups like ISIS to Carry out Attacks in Europe*. Retrieved 2017, from uk.businessinsider.com: http://uk.businessinsider.com/how-much-do-terrorist-attacks-cost-deutsche-bank-2016-12.

Matthew, L. (2015, February). *Hezbollah Finances: Funding the Party of God.* Retrieved 01 09, 2018, from The Washington Institute.org:http://www.wa shingtoninstitute.org/policy-analysis/view/hezbollah-finances-funding-the-party-of-god

McCory, T. (2014, June 12). *ISIS Just Stole $425 million Iraqi Governor Says and Became the 'World's Richest Terrorist Group'.* Retrieved 2017, from The Washington Post: https://www.washingtonpost.com/news/morning-mix/ wp/2014/06/12/isis-just-stole-425-million-and-became-the-worlds-richest-terrorist-group/?utm_term=.b8f9ae5cf0c8

MEMRI. (2017). *ISIS 'Rumiyah' Magazine in French: Anyone Who Participates in Elections is an Infidel; Muslims in France Should Achieve Martyrdom by Killing Candidates and Burning Polling Stations.* MEMRI JTTM.

MENAFATF. (2017). *Middle East and North Africa Financial Action Task Force.* Retrieved 07 20, 2017, from Middle east and North Africa Financial Action Task Force: http://www.menafatf.org/about

Milliyet. (2013, May 9). *İşte Lavrion Kampı.* Retrieved 26.08.2017, from milliyet. com.tr: http://www.milliyet.com.tr/iste-lavrion-kampi/dunya/detay/1705944/ default.htm

Money Jihad. (2013, January 7). *Sharia Banks that Fund Terrorism.* Retrieved 03 25, 2017, from Money Jihad Combatting Terrorist Financing: https://money jihad.wordpress.com/2013/01/07/sharia-banks-that-fund-terrorism/

MONEYVAL. (2017). *Committee of Experts on the Evaluation of Anti-Money Laundering Measures and the Financing of Terrorism.* Retrieved 07 20, 2017, from Council of Europe: http://www.coe.int/en/web/moneyval/

MONEYVAL COMMITTEE – Council of Europe. (2012). *Criminal Money Flows on the Internet: Methods, Trends and Multi-Stakeholder Counteraction.* MONEYVAL Committee, Strasbourg, Council of Europe.

Moore, J. (2017, August 17). *Barcelona Attack Live Updates: Van Plows into Crowd on Famous Las Ramblas.* Retrieved 2018, from newsweek.com:http://www. newsweek.com/barcelona-crash-live-updates-van-plows-crowd-famous-las-ramblas-651914

Nashabe, O. (2012, May 4). *China's Ambassador in Lebanon: Hezbollah Arms a Trade Matter.* Retrieved 01 16, 2018, from Al-Akhbar: http://english.al-akhbar. com/node/6964

Norges offentlige utredninger. (2012). *Rapport fra 22: Juli-kommisjonen.* Oslo: Norges offentlige utredninger.

Nyheter, D. (2013, February 18). *Självmordsbombaren fick 750.000 från CSN.* Retrieved 2017, from dn.se:https://www.dn.se/nyheter/sverige/sjalvmords bombaren-fick-750000-fran-csn/

O'Connor, W. (2017, June 4). *Timeline of Europe's Terror Attacks*. Retrieved 01 18, 2018, from Independent.ie: https://www.independent.ie/world-news/europe/timeline-of-europes-terror-attacks-35786085.html

Oftendal, E. (2015). *The Financing of Jihadi Terrorist Cells in Europe*. Oslo: Norwegian Defence Research Establishment (FFI).

Osborn, A. (2015, July 2). *Islamic State Looting Syrian, Iraqi Sites on Industrial Scale: UNESCO*. Retrieved 01 17, 2018, from Reuters: https://uk.reuters.com/article/uk-mideast-crisis-unesco/islamic-state-looting-syrian-iraqi-sites-on-industrial-scale-unesco-idUKKCN0PC1OS20150702

Ozcan, N. (1999). *PKK*. Ankara: Asam.

Ozdemir, H., & Pekgozlu, I. (2012). Where do Terror Organization Get Their Money? A Case Study: Financial Resources of PKK. *International Journal of Security and Terroism*, Vol. 3, No. 2, 85–102.

Ozkan, O. (2016). Money Laundering Activities of the PKK. *Mile East Review of Public Administration (MERPA)*, Vol. 2, No. 1, 1–10.

Ozturk, Y. N. (2017). *Kuran-ı Kerim Meali*. Yeni Boyut Istanbul.

Passeri, P. (2017, January 19). *2016 Cyber Attacks Statistics*. Retrieved 12 11, 2017, from HACKMAGEDDON: http://www.hackmageddon.com/2017/01/19/2016-cyber-attacks-statistics/

Patrick, J. M., & Harjit, S. S. (2005). *The Hawala Alternative Remittance System and its Role in Money Laundering*. Washington: Financial Crimes Enforcement Network (FinCEN).

Perspektif, H. (2016, November 25). *PKK'nın Para Kaynagi Almaya*. Retrieved 10 28, 2017, from haber.akademicperspektif.com: http://haber.akademikperspektif.com/2016/11/25/pkknin-para-kaynagi-almanya/

Polat, A. (2009). Katılım Bankacılığı: Dünya Uygulamalarına İlişkin Sorunlar-Fırsatlar; Türkiye İçin Projeksiyonlar. In A. Yabanlı, *Finansal Yenilik ve Açılımları ile Katılım Bankacılığı* (Vol. 1, pp. 77–120). İstanbul: Türkiye Katılım Bankaları Birliği.

Prasad, N. (2016). *The Financing of Terrorism*. Delhi: Alpha Editions.

Qorchi, M. El., Maimbo, S. M., & Wilson, J. F. (2003). *Informal Funds Transfer Systems: An Analysis of the Informal Hawala System*. Washington: International Monetary Fund.

Rajder, A. (1995). Odzemanjeto na profit od korupcija. *Bezbednost* Volume.1, 28.

Ranstorp, M. (2011). Terrorist Awakening in Sweden? *Combating Terrorism Center CTC SENTINEL*, Vol. 4, No. 1, 1–24.

Rumiyah. (2017, May). *The Ruling on the Belligerent Christians*. Retrieved from Rumiyah: https://azelin.files.wordpress.com/2017/05/romemagazine-9.pdf.

Ryder, N. (2015). *The Financial War on Terrorism* (Vol. 1). New York: Routledge.

SABAH. (2015, September 5). *PKK, göçmenlerin yılda 300 milyon $'ını çalıyor!* Retrieved 10 28, 2017, from sabah.com.tr: https://www.sabah.com.tr/gun dem/2015/09/05/pkk-gocmenlerin-yilda-300-milyon-ini-caliyor?paging=6.

sakerhetspolisen. (2014, October 22). *Förundersökning om terrordåd nedlagd.* Retrieved 24.07.2017, from sakerhetspolisen.se:http://www.sakerhetspolisen. se/publikationer/fallstudier-och-artiklar-fran-arsbocker/terrorism/forunder sokning-om-terrordad-nedlagd.html.

Shatz, A. (2004). *In Search of Hezbollah.* New York: The New York Review of Books.

Simpson, G. R. (2007, July 26). *U.S. Tracks Saudi Bank Favored by Extremists.* Retrieved 03 15, 2017, from *The Wall Street Journal*:https://www.wsj.com/ articles/SB118530038250476405

Sirgany, Z. S. (2017, August 29). *Hezbollah: Mission Accomplished Against ISIS in Lebanon.* Retrieved 01 09, 2018, from CNN.com:http://edition.cnn. com/2017/08/29/middleeast/hezbollah-isis/index.html

Solomon, E., & Jones, S. (2015, December 14). *ISIS Inc: Loot and Taxes Keep Jihadi Ecomony Churning.* Retrieved 01 10, 2018, from Financial Times.com: https://www.ft.com/content/aee89a00-9ff1-11e5-beba-5e33e2b79e46

Staff, T. T. (2015, November 16). *Russia says "Hezbollah, Hamas not terror groups".* Retrieved 01 07, 2018, from *The Times of Israel*: https://www.timesof israel.com/russia-says-hezbollah-hamas-not-terror-groups/

Stefan, H., Peter, N. R., John, H.-M., &Rajan, B. (2017). *Caliphate in Decline: An Estimate of Islamic State's Financial Fortunes.* London: The International Centre for the Study of Radicalization and Political Violence, King's College.

Stewart, S. (2010, March 13). *Setting the Record Straight on Grassroots Jihadism.* Retrieved 01 20, 2018, from worldview.stratfor.com: https://worldview.strat for.com/article/setting-record-straight-grassroots-jihadism#axzz3Hhj09uDJ.

Stewart, S. (2013, December 19). *Gauging the Jihadist Movement, Part 1: The Goals of the Jihadists.* Retrieved 02 01, 2018, from worldview.stratfor. com:https://worldview.stratfor.com/article/gauging-jihadist-movement-part-1-goals-jihadists#axzz3Hhj09uDJ

Studies, A. C. (2017). *Setbacks and Realignments: The Continuing Evolution of Militant Islamist Groups in Africa.* Africa: Center for Strategic Studies.

Sulejmanov, Z. (2000). *Makedonska Kriminologija.* Skopje: Grafohartija Skopje.

Taseva, S. (2003). *Perenje Pari.* Skopje: Data Pons Skopje.

Taylor, M. (2008, December 17). *The Doctor, the Engineer and a Failed Call That Averted Disaster.* Retrieved 2017, from The Guardian.com:http://www.the guardian.com/uk/2008/dec/17/glasgow-airport-trial-uk-security.

Terrell, R. G. (2007). *Islamic Banking Financing Terrorism or Meeting Economic Demand?* Retrieved from Dudley Knox Library: https://calhoun.nps.edu/handle/10945/3013

The Council of Europe. (1977). *European Convention on the Suppression of Terrorism.* Retrieved 03 20, 2017, from The Council of Europe:https://rm.coe.int/16800771b2

The Council of Europe. (1990). *Convention on Laundering, Search, Seizure and Confiscation of the Proceeds from Crime.* Retrieved 05 16, 2017, from The Council of Europe: https://rm.coe.int/168007bd23

The Council of Europe. (2003). *Protocol Amending the European Convention on the Suppression of Terrorism.* Retrieved 03 20, 2017, from The Council of Europe: https://rm.coe.int/168008370d

The Council of Europe. (2005a). *Council of Europe Convention on the Prevention of Terrorism.* Retrieved 04 15, 2017, from The Council of Europe: https://rm.coe.int/168008371c

The Council of Europe. (2005b). *Council of Europe Convention on Laundering, Search, Seizure and Confiscation of the Proceeds from Crime and on the Financing of Terrorism.* Retrieved 04 15, 2017, from The Council of Europe: https://rm.coe.int/168008371f

The Council of Europe. (2015). *Additional Protocol to the Council of Europe Convention on the Prevention of Terrorism (Adopted by the Committee of Ministers at its 125th Session on 19 May 2015).* Retrieved 05 10, 2017, from The Council of Europe:http://www.un.org/en/sc/ctc/docs/2015/Additional%20Protocol%20to%20the%20Council%20of%20Europe%20Convention%20on%20the%20Prevention%20of%20Terrorism.pdf

The New York Times. (2011, December 13). *Money Laundering at Lebanese Bank.* Retrieved 10.01.2018, from The New York Times.com: http://www.nytimes.com/interactive/2011/12/13/world/middleeast/lebanese-money-laundering.html

Torsha, G., & Pooja, B., Dr. (2012). Analysis of Rumiyah Magazine. *IOSR Journal of Humanities and Social Science* Vol. 22, No. 7, Ver.12, 16–22.

Treasury, U. D. (1995). *Terrorist Assets Report to the Congress on Assets Belonging to Terrorist Countries or International Terrorist Organization.* Washington: US Department of the Treasury.

UN Convention. (1988). *United Nations Convention Against Illicit Traffic in Narcotic Drugs and Psychotropic Substances.* Retrieved 05 20, 2017, from UNODC: https://www.unodc.org/pdf/convention_1988_en.pdf

UN Resolution 54/109. (1999). *International Convention for the Suppression of the Financing of Terrorism.* Retrieved 05 15, 2017, from United Nations: http://www.un.org/law/cod/finterr.htm

UN Security Council. (2002). *Terrorism Financing*. New York: UN.

United Nation Security Council. (2016). *Report of the Secretary-General on the Threat Posed by ISIL (Da'esh) to International Peace and Security and the Range of United Nations Efforts in Support of Member States in Countering the Threat.* New York: United Nation Security Council.

UNODC. (2004). *United Nations Convention Against Transnational Organized Crime and the Protocols Thereto.* Retrieved 05 10, 2017, from https://www.unodc.org/documents/treaties/UNTOC/Publications/TOC%20Convention/TOCebook-e.pdf

UNODC. (2016). *World Drug Report*. New York: UNDOC.

UNSC. (2001a). *UNSC Resolution 1368.* Retrieved 04 15, 2017, from United Nations: https://documents-dds-ny.un.org/doc/UNDOC/GEN/N01/533/82/PDF/N0153382.pdf?OpenElement

UNSC. (2001b). *UNSC Resolution 1373.* Retrieved 05 15, 2017, from United Nations: https://documents-dds-ny.un.org/doc/UNDOC/GEN/N01/557/43/PDF/N0155743.pdf?OpenElement

UNSC. (2017). *Resolutions.* Retrieved 04 15, 2017, from United Nations Security Council Subsidiary Organs.

UNSC Counter Terrorism Committee. (2017). *Security Council Counter Terrorism Committee-Homepage.* Retrieved 05 01, 2017, from Security Council Counter Terrorism Committee: https://www.un.org/sc/ctc/.

Wagner, V. (2017, September 5). *Germany: Terror Casualty Hanns Martin Schleyer – Sacrifice by the State.* Retrieved 01 18, 2018, from dw.com: http://www.dw.com/en/germany-terror-casualty-hanns-martin-schleyer-sacrificed-by-the-state/a-40340024.

Wikipedia. (2015). *HAMAS.* Retrieved 01 18, 2018, from Wikipedia: https://en.wikipedia.org/wiki/Hamas.

Yatbaz, A. (2015). Faizsiz Finansal Kuruluşlarda Zekât, Zekât Fonu ve Zekât Muhasebesi. *International Journal of Islamic Economics and Finance Studies,* Vol. 1, No. 2, 113–139.